The
OXFORD
Illustrated
Junior Dictionary

Compiled by
Rosemary Sansome, Dee Reid

Illustrated by
Barry Rowe

D1390112

OXFORD UNIVERSITY PRESS

Oxford University Press, Walton Street, Oxford OX2 6DP

Oxford New York
Athens Auckland Bangkok Bombay
Calcutta Cape Town Dar es Salaam Delhi
Florence Hong Kong Istanbul Karachi
Kuala Lumpur Madras Madrid Melbourne
Mexico City Nairobi Paris Singapore
Taipei Tokyo Toronto

and associated companies in
Berlin Ibadan

Oxford is a trade mark of Oxford University Press

First published 1989
Redesigned impression 1994
10 9 8 7 6 5 4

ISBN 0 19 910331 3 (paperback)
ISBN 0 19 910330 5 (hardback)

A CIP catalogue record for this book is available
from the British Library.

Printed in Hong Kong

Contents

A a

abbey 1 a big, old church once used by monks or nuns
Westminster Abbey
2 a place where monks or nuns live and work

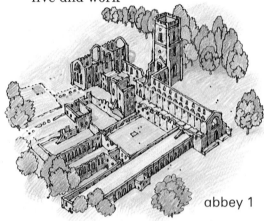

abbey 1

abbreviation a short way of writing a word or a group of words. P.T.O. is an abbreviation for *please turn over.*

ability the power to do something
He has the ability to speak six languages.

able having the power to do something
She is able to sing high notes.

aboard on or onto a ship, bus, train, or aeroplane
All aboard!

about 1 almost
It's about four o'clock.
2 that tells you something
a book about ships
3 in any direction
rushing about

above 1 overhead
the sky above
2 higher than
The aeroplane flew above the clouds.

abroad in another country
a holiday abroad

abrupt sudden

absent not in a place
absent from school

accelerator one of the pedals in a car. The driver presses it with his foot to make the car go faster.

accent the way people say their words
Australians have a different accent from Americans.

accept to take what is offered to you

accident 1 something bad that happens and is not meant to happen
He broke his leg in a bicycle accident.
2 *by accident* by chance
We met by accident.

accompany 1 to go with someone
He accompanied her on the journey to Paris.
2 to play the piano or guitar while someone sings or dances

account 1 a story about something that has happened
There was an account of the football match in the local paper.
2 a list that tells you how much money you owe or have spent
a bank account

accurate correct and exact

accuse to say that someone has done something wrong
The policeman accused him of stealing the car.

ace a card used in a game, marked to show it is number one. A pack of cards has four aces in it.

ache to have a pain that goes on hurting
My head is aching.

achievement   something difficult or special that you have done
Winning the medal was a great achievement for Jim.

acid   a kind of liquid that can burn your skin. Lemons contain a very weak acid.

acorn   the nut of an oak tree

acrobat   someone who does exciting jumping and balancing tricks to entertain people

across   from one side to the other
I swam across the river.

act   **1** to take part in a play
2 to do something
The girl acted quickly and was able to save the drowning man.

action   **1** doing something
2 something that is done

active   busy or working

activity   **1** an action or occupation
2 something for you to do
The sports activities on offer at school include netball and football.

actor   a man who acts in a play

actress   a woman who acts in a play

actual   real

add   **1** to put with something else to make it bigger
Add another brick to the tower.
2 to find the answer to a sum like this 3 + 3 =

adder   a small snake with poisonous teeth

addition   **1** adding numbers
2 something that is added
The addition of the curtains made the room much brighter.

additional   extra

address   the number of the house and the names of the street and town where someone lives

adjective   any word that tells you what someone or something is like
Beautiful, tall, nasty, delicious, and *difficult* are all adjectives.

admiral   a very important officer in the navy

admire   **1** to think someone or something is very good
The teacher admired his work.
2 to look at something and enjoy it
They were admiring the view.

admission   the cost of being allowed to go in

admit   **1** to let someone come in
No child under ten years of age can be admitted.
2 to say you were the person who did something wrong
He admitted that he stole the jewels.

adopt   to take someone into your family as your own child

adore   to like very much

adult   someone who is fully grown

advance   to move forward

advantage   something that helps you to do better than other people
an unfair advantage

adventure   something exciting that happens to you

adverb   any word that tells you how, when, or where something happens
Away, often, somewhere, now, slowly, and *quickly* are all adverbs.

advertisements   words or pictures that try to make you buy something

advice   what is said to someone to help them decide what to do
My advice is save your money.

advise   to tell someone what you think it would be best for them to do
The doctor advised the girl to rest.

aerial   wires or metal rods for picking up or sending out radio and television programmes

aeroplane   a flying machine with wings and an engine

affect   to make someone or something different in some way
Her handwriting was affected by her sore finger.

affection   the feeling you have for someone or something you like a lot
Most children have a great affection for their pets.

afford   to have enough money to pay for something

afraid   frightened

after   **1** later than
You finished after me.
2 following
Dad went to sleep after dinner.

afternoon   the time from the middle of the day until about six o'clock

afterwards   later

again   once more
Try again!

against   **1** on the opposite side to
We played against your team and won.
2 on or next to
He leant against the wall.

age   how old someone or something is

agent   someone whose job is to arrange things for people
a travel agent

agile   able to move quickly and easily

agree   to think the same as someone else

aground   trapped on sand and rocks in shallow water. Ships sometimes run aground on rocks and are badly damaged.

ahead   in front
I went on ahead to open the gate.

aid   **1** to help
We sent blankets to aid the victims of the earthquake.
2 something that helps
a hearing aid

aim   **1** to point a gun at something
She aimed the gun at the target.
2 to throw, kick, or shoot at something you are trying to hit
He aimed the ball into the far corner of the net.
3 to try to do something
They aimed to finish in time for tea.

air   what everyone breathes

aircraft   any aeroplane or helicopter
two aircraft

air force   a group of people trained to use aeroplanes for fighting

air-gun   a gun that uses air instead of an explosive to make the bullets shoot out

air-hostess   a woman whose job is to look after people travelling in an aeroplane

airport   a place where people can get on or off aeroplanes

air-tight   tightly closed so that air cannot get into it or out of it
an air-tight jar

aisle   (*say* ile *to rhyme with* tile) a path between groups of seats. Churches, cinemas, aeroplanes, and buses have aisles.

alarm   **1** a sudden, frightened feeling
She cried out in alarm when she heard the strange noise.
2 a warning sound or sign
a clock with an alarm

album   a book where you can keep things like stamps or photographs

alcohol   a liquid that has no colour. One kind of alcohol is found in certain drinks, such as beer and whisky.

alert   lively and ready for anything

alight   on fire

alive   living

all   **1** everyone or everything
Let's start singing. All together now . . .
2 the whole of something
He's eaten all the cake.

alley   a very narrow street

alligator   a large animal that lives in rivers in America and China. It has short legs, a long body, and sharp teeth.

allotment   a small piece of land that you pay to use. People grow vegetables, fruit, and flowers on their allotments.

allow   to let something happen
Are you allowed to watch that programme?

all right   **1** safe and well
2 I agree
All right, you can stay up.

ally   a person or country fighting on the same side

almond   a kind of flat nut with a very hard shell

almonds

almost   very nearly
We're almost home now.

alone   without others
She's working alone in the corner.

along   **1** from one end to the other
He ran along the top of the wall.
2 *Come along!* Hurry up!

aloud   in a voice that can be heard
Do not read to yourself – read aloud.

alphabet   all the letters used in writing a language, arranged in order

АБВГДЕЖЗИЙКЛМНОПР
СТУФХЦЧШЩЪЫЬЭЮЯ

ض ط ظ ع غ ف ق ك ل م ن ه و ي
ا ب ت ث ج ح خ د ذ ر ز س ش

ΑΒΓΔΕΖΗΘΙΚΛΜΝ
ΞΟΠΡΣΤΥΦΧΨΩ

अ आ इ ई उ ऊ ऋ ए ऐ ओ औ क ख ग घ ङ
च छ ज झ ञ ट ठ ड ढ ण त थ द ध न
प फ ब भ म य र ल व श ष स ह

alphabets

already   **1** by this time
He was already there when we arrived.
2 before now
I've already done that.

also   as well
jelly and also ice-cream

altar   the table with a cross on it in a church

alter   to change

alteration   a change in someone or something
They had to make alterations to the uniform as it was too big for her.

although   though

altogether   counting everything or everyone

aluminium   a very light metal, coloured like silver

always   at all times
He's always hungry.

amateur   **1** someone who does something as a hobby
2 someone who takes part in a sport and is not paid

a b c d e f g h i j k l m n o p q r s t u v w x y z

amaze   to surprise greatly
She amazed her friends by coming to school in a helicopter.

ambition   something that you want to do very much
Her ambition is to be a doctor.

ambulance   a van for taking injured or ill people to hospital

ammunition   anything that is fired from a gun

among   in the middle of

amount   how much or how many there are
a large amount of money

amuse   **1** to make someone laugh or smile
2 to make time pass pleasantly for someone
I was amusing myself with this puzzle.

amusement   **1** an amused feeling
They watched in amusement as the baby took its first steps.
2 something that entertains you

ancestor   a member of the same family who lived long ago

anchor   a heavy metal hook joined to a ship by a chain. It is dropped into the sea, where it digs into the bottom to keep the ship still.

ancient   very old
This church is ancient – it was built hundreds of years ago.

angel   a messenger sent by God

anger   a strong feeling that you get when you are not pleased. It makes you want to fight or hurt someone.
She was filled with anger when she saw them teasing the cat.

angle   the corner where two lines meet

angler   a fisherman who uses a rod, hook, and line

angry   feeling anger

animal   anything that lives and can move about. Birds, fish, snakes, wasps, and elephants are all animals

ankle   the thin part of the leg where it is joined to the foot

anniversary   a day when you remember something special that happened on the same day in another year
a wedding anniversary

announce   to say something in front of a lot of people
They announced the winner of the competition.

annoy   to make someone angry

annual   **1** a book that comes out once a year
2 happening every year
an annual meeting

anorak   a waterproof jacket with a hood

another   **1** a different one
Choose another hat – that one is too big.
2 one more
No, you can't have another cake.

9

answer **1** to say something to someone who has asked you a question
What is 6 × 7? Can anyone answer?
2 something that is said or done in return
Do you think you will get an answer to your letter?

ant a tiny insect

Antarctic the very cold sea and land in the south of the world

antelope a wild animal that looks like a deer. Antelopes are found in Africa and parts of Asia.

antique (*say* an-teek) something old that is often very valuable

anxious worried
She was anxious when he was late home.

any **1** some
Have you any wool?
2 at all
Are you any better?

anybody, anyone any person

anything any thing
It's so dark, I can't see anything.

anywhere in any place

apart away from each other
London and Sydney are far apart.

ape an animal like a large monkey with long arms and no tail. Chimpanzees and gorillas are apes.

apologize to say that you are sorry for doing something wrong

apparatus special things that you use for doing something
P.E. apparatus

appeal to ask for something that you need
He appealed for help.

appear **1** to come and be seen
He appeared from behind the curtain.
2 to seem
It appears to be the wrong size.

appearance **1** what someone looks like
His appearance was very untidy.
2 coming so that you can be seen
The appearance of the rabbit surprised everyone.

appendix the small tube inside the body that sometimes causes an illness called **appendicitis**

appetite the wish for food
She's been ill and has no appetite.

applaud to clap to show that you are pleased

applause clapping

apple a round, crisp, juicy fruit

appoint to choose someone for a job
A new headmistress was appointed.

appointment a time when you have arranged to go and see someone
an appointment at the dentist's

approach to come near to

approximate nearly correct

apricot   a round, soft, juicy fruit. It has a large stone in it and a thin, orange skin.

apron   something worn over the front of the body to keep the clothes underneath clean

aqualung   a cylinder filled with air and joined to a tube. People strap aqualungs on their backs so that they can breathe under water.

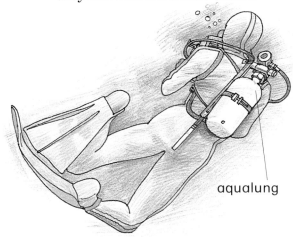

aqualung

aquarium   a large, glass container where fish are kept

arch   a curved part that helps to support a bridge or building

archery   shooting at a target with a bow and arrow

architect   (*say* arkitect) a person who draws plans for buildings

Arctic   the very cold sea and land in the north of the world

area   **1** an amount of surface
The area of a field is calculated by multiplying the length by the breadth.
2 a part of a country or place
a no-smoking area

argue   to talk about something with people who do not agree with you

argument   talking in an angry or excited way to someone who does not agree with you

arithmetic   finding out about numbers

arm   the part of the body between the shoulder and the hand

armchair   a comfortable chair with parts at the side for you to rest your arms on

armour   **1** metal clothes worn in battles long ago
2 sheets of metal put round ships and tanks to protect them in war

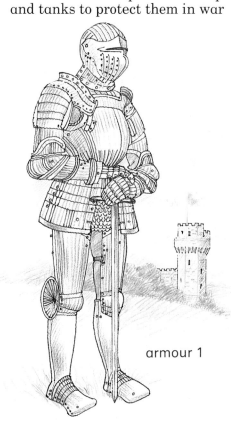

armour 1

armpit   the part underneath the top of the arm

arms   weapons

army   a large group of people trained to fight on land

11

around   1 all round
Around the castle there was a thick forest.
2 here and there
Look around for it.

arouse   to wake someone up

arrange   to put in order
Arrange the books in neat piles.

arrangement   something that it has been decided will happen
We made an arrangement to meet after school.

arrest   to take someone prisoner
The policeman arrested the thief.

arrive   to come to the end of a journey

arrow   a pointed stick that is shot from a bow

art   1 drawing and painting
2 the ability to do something difficult

article   a particular thing
A skirt is an article of clothing.

artificial   not natural because it has been made by people or machines
artificial flowers

artist   someone who draws or paints pictures

ascend   (*say* a-send)
to go up

ash   1 the grey powder left when something has been burned
2 a kind of tree (See picture on p. 219)

ashamed   feeling very sorry and guilty about something

ashore   on land
The sailors went ashore.

aside   to one side
Stand aside!

ask   to speak in order to find out or get something

asleep   sleeping

aspirin   a small white pill. You swallow it when you have a cold, or a pain, to make you feel better.

ass   a donkey

assembly   the time when the whole school meets together

assembly line   a group of people working to put something together in a factory

assist   to help

assistance   help

assistant   1 someone whose job is to help someone more important
an assistant to the manager
2 someone who serves in a shop

assorted   with different sorts put together
a bag of assorted sweets

asthma   an illness that makes breathing difficult

astonish   to surprise greatly

astonishment   great surprise
They stared in astonishment at the spaceship.

astronaut   someone who travels in space

astronomer   someone who studies the sun, the stars, and the planets

astronomy   finding out about the sun, the stars, and the planets

ate   see **eat**

athlete   someone who trains to be good at running, jumping, or throwing

atlas   a book of maps

atmosphere   the air around the earth

atom   one of the very tiny things that everything is made up of

attach   to join or fasten
You must attach a label to your suitcase.

attack   to start fighting in order to beat or hurt someone

attempt   to try
He attempted to jump over the gate.

attend   **1** to be in a place in order to take part in something
She was asked to attend a meeting after school.
2 to listen carefully
You should attend to what the teacher says.

attendance   being at a place in order to take part in something
school attendance

attention   **1** careful listening, reading, or thinking
2 *pay attention* take notice

attic   a room or rooms inside the roof of a house

attract   **1** to interest
The toy attracted the baby's attention and he stopped crying.
2 to make something come nearer
The magnet attracted the small piece of metal.

attractive   very pleasant to look at

auction   (*say* oction)
a sale where things are sold to the people who offer the most money for them

audience   people who have come to a place to see or hear something

aunt   your uncle's wife or the sister of one of your parents

author   someone who writes books or stories

authority   the power to make other people do as you say
The police have the authority to stop speeding cars.

autograph   your name written by yourself

automatic   able to work on its own and control itself. Slot machines are automatic.

autumn   the part of the year when leaves fall off the trees and it gets colder

available   ready for you to use
In winter, sledges are available in the shops.

avalanche   a large amount of snow, rock, or ice sliding suddenly down a mountain

avenue   a road, often with trees along each side

average   ordinary or usual
average marks
of average height for his age

avoid   to keep out of the way of someone or something

await   to wait for

awake   not sleeping

award   a prize that you have worked for
There is an award for the neatest writing.

aware   knowing about something
She was aware that if she were late home her mother would worry.

away   **1** not here
She was away yesterday.
2 to another place
He ran away.

awful   very bad

awkward   **1** clumsy
2 difficult to deal with
an awkward customer
3 not convenient
an awkward time

axe   a tool for chopping

axle   a rod that goes through the centre of wheels to join them to something
the car axle

B b

baby   a very young child

bachelor   a man who has not married

back   **1** the side opposite the front
2 the part of the body between the neck and the bottom or tail

backward, backwards
1 towards the back
2 in the opposite way to usual

bacon   dried or salty meat from a pig's back or sides

badge   something worn pinned or stitched to clothes. It shows which group someone belongs to or how important he is.
a school badge, a sheriff's badge

badger   a grey animal that digs holes in the ground. It has a white face with black stripes on it.

badgers

baggage   luggage, suitcases

bail   **1** one of the two pieces of wood put on top of the stumps in cricket
2 to throw water out of a boat, using buckets
Bail out the water before we sink.

bait   food put on a hook or in a trap to catch animals

bake   to cook inside an oven

baker   someone whose job is to make or sell bread and cakes

balance   **1** a pair of scales for weighing things
2 to keep or make something steady
The seal is balancing a ball on the end of its nose.

balcony **1** a platform with a rail round it outside an upstairs window
2 the seats upstairs in a cinema or theatre

bald without any hair on the head

bale **1** a large bundle or package
a bale of hay
2 *to bale out* to jump out of an aeroplane with a parachute

ball **1** a round object used in games
2 a big party with a lot of dancing

ballerina a woman who is a ballet dancer

ballet a story told on the stage in dancing, mime, and music

balloon **1** a small, coloured, rubber bag that you can blow up and burst
2 a bag filled with hot air or gas so that it floats in the sky

balloon 2

bamboo a tall plant with stiff, hollow stems. It grows in very hot countries and is used for making furniture.

ban to say that someone must never do a certain thing
They have banned roller-skating in the playground.

banana a long fruit with a thick yellow skin

band **1** a group of people
a band of robbers
2 some people playing musical instruments together
3 a strip of material. Bands are put round things to decorate them or to keep them together.
a rubber band

bandage a strip of material for wrapping round part of the body that has been hurt

bandit an outlaw who is a robber

bang **1** the sudden, loud, hard sound an explosion makes
2 to hit or shut with a loud noise
Don't bang the door!

bangle a ring worn round the arm

banish to send someone away from a place as a punishment
The wicked king banished the princess from the land for seven years.

banisters the posts and rail at the side of a staircase

banjo a musical instrument with strings that you play with your fingers. It is smaller and rounder than a guitar.

bank **1** a place that looks after money and valuable things for people
2 the ground near the edge of a river, canal, or lake

banner a kind of flag

banquet   a big feast given by someone important

bar   **1** a long piece of wood or metal
2 a block of chocolate, toffee, or soap
3 a place that serves food and drinks at a counter
a coffee bar

barbed wire   wire with sharp spikes in it, used for making fences

barber   a man whose job is to cut mens' and boys' hair

bare   without any clothes or covering

bargain   **1** a promise to give something in return for something else
They made a bargain to swap the toys.
2 something that costs much less than usual
You can get bargains at jumble sales.

barge   a long boat with a flat bottom. Barges are used on canals and rivers.

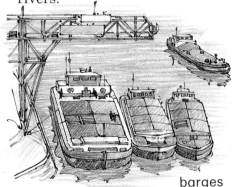

barges

bark   **1** to make the hard, loud sound a dog makes
2 the hard covering round a tree's trunk and branches

barley   a plant grown by farmers. Its seed is used for making food and beer. (See picture on p. 218)

barn   a large building on a farm, where things are stored

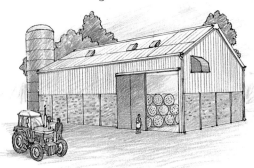

barracks   an army building where soldiers live together

barrel   **1** a round, wooden container with flat ends
a barrel of beer
2 the part like a tube at the front of a gun

barren   without plants
barren land

barrier   a fence or something that stands in the way

barrow   a small cart that is pushed

base   the bottom part of something
The base of the statue was made of wood.

basement   the rooms in a building that are below the ground

bash   to hit very hard

bashful   shy

basic   most important
basic information

basin   a bowl

basket   a bag made of straw or cane

bat   **1** an animal like a mouse with wings
2 a piece of wood for hitting a ball in a game
3 to have a turn at playing with a bat in a game like cricket

batch   a number of things together
a batch of letters

bath   **1** a large container filled with water. You sit in it and wash yourself all over.
2 to put a baby or animal in water and wash it
Bath the muddy puppy.

bathe   **1** to play or swim in the sea or a river
They bathed in the pool.
2 to wash part of yourself carefully and gently
He bathed his cut finger.

bathroom   the room where you can have a bath or wash

batsman   the person who uses the bat in cricket or rounders

batter   **1** a liquid made from flour, egg, and milk. It is used for making pancakes and frying fish.
2 to damage something by hitting it often
The wind battered down the fence.

battery   a closed container with electricity inside it. You put batteries inside things like torches and radios to make them work.

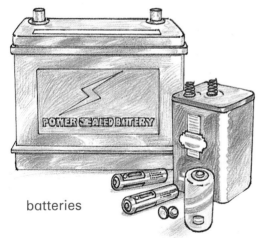

batteries

battle   fighting between groups of people

bawl   to shout or cry loudly
The hungry baby was bawling.

bay   a place where the coast bends inwards and sea fills the space

bayonet   a sharp blade that can be fixed to a gun

bazaar   a group of stalls selling different things to get money for something
a church bazaar

BBC   short for **British Broadcasting Corporation**

beach   land by the edge of the sea. It is usually covered with sand or small stones.

bead   a small, round object with a hole through the middle. Beads are threaded on string to make necklaces and bracelets.

beak   the hard part round a bird's mouth

beaker   a kind of tall cup. Some beakers have no handle.

beam   **1** a long piece of wood
2 a line of light
the torch beam
3 to smile very happily

bean   a vegetable. Beans are round seeds and some sorts grow inside long green pods that can also be eaten.
French beans, broad beans

beans

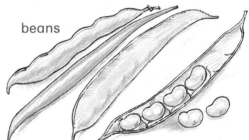

beanbag   a small cloth bag filled with dried beans, used in games

bear **1** to carry
The donkey bore the load patiently.
2 to put up with
He could not have borne any more pain.
3 to give birth to
Their baby was born yesterday.
4 a large animal with very thick fur

bear 4

beard hair growing on a man's chin

beast **1** any big animal
2 a horrible person

beat **1** to do better than someone else
You beat me last time.
2 to hit often
The horse had been beaten with a stick.
3 to stir very hard

beautiful **1** very attractive
a beautiful face
2 very pleasant
a beautiful day

beauty something or someone beautiful

became see **become**

because for the reason that
I got wet because it rained.

beckon to move your hand to show someone that you want them to come nearer

become to come to be
It suddenly became very dark.

bedroom the room where you sleep

bee an insect that can fly, sting, and make honey

beech a kind of tree
(See picture on p. 219)

beef meat from a cow, bull, or ox

beehive a kind of box for keeping bees in

beer a strong brown drink

beetle an insect with hard wing cases

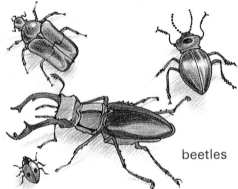

beetles

beetroot a round, dark red vegetable

before **1** earlier than
I was here before you.
2 in front of
It vanished before my eyes.

began see **begin**

beggar someone who lives by asking other people for money, clothes, or food

begin to start
I'm beginning to understand.
He began school last week.
I have begun to learn the piano.

beginner   someone who has just started learning something

beginning   the start of something

begun   see **begin**

behave   **1** to show good or bad manners in front of other people
He's behaved badly, she's behaving well.
2 *Behave yourself!* Be good!

behaviour   how you behave

behind   at the back of
He hid behind the wall.

belief   what someone believes

believe   to feel sure that something is true

bell   a hollow piece of metal that rings when it is hit

bells

bellow   to shout and make a lot of noise like an angry bull

belly   the stomach

belong   **1** to be someone's
That pen belongs to me.
2 to be part of something
to belong to the Scouts
3 to be in the proper place
Your coat belongs on the peg, not on the floor.

below   underneath
Write your address below your name.

belt   a stiff band worn round the waist

bench   a wooden or stone seat for more than one person

bend   **1** to make something curved or not straight
2 to lean over so that your head is nearer to the ground
He bent down and looked at his shoes.

beneath   underneath

bent   see **bend**

berry   any small, round fruit with seeds in it. Some berries are poisonous.

beside   at the side of
a house beside the sea

besides   as well as
Ten people besides me also won prizes.

best   better than any other
my best friend

betray   **1** to give away a secret
2 to give information about your friends or country to the enemy
A spy betrays his country's secrets.

better   **1** more able
better than me at swimming
2 well again
I'm better now, thank you.

between   **1** in the middle of two people or things
I sat between Mum and Dad.
2 among
Share the money between you.

beware   be careful
Beware of the dog.

bewildered   very puzzled

bewitched   under a spell

beyond   further than
Don't go beyond the end of the road.

Bible   the holy book that is read in all Christian churches

bicycle, bike   a machine with two wheels and pedals, that you can ride (See picture on p. 214)

bill   **1** a piece of paper that tells you how much money you owe
He paid all his bills.
2 a bird's beak

billiards   a game played on a long table with rods used to hit three small balls

billy-goat   a male goat

bind   to tie together
The prisoner's hands were bound behind his back.

bingo   a game where each person has a card with different numbers on it. Each player marks the numbers off when they are called.

binoculars   a special pair of glasses like two tubes joined together. When you look through them, things far away seem much nearer.

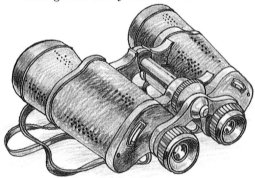

bird   any animal with feathers, wings, and a beak

birth   the beginning of life, when a baby leaves its mother and starts to breathe

birthday   the day each year when you remember the day someone was born

biscuit   a kind of small, thin, dry cake

bishop   a priest who is in charge of other priests

bit   **1** a very small amount of something
2 the part of a bridle that goes into a horse's mouth
3 see **bite**

bitch   a female dog

bite   to use the teeth to cut into something
Your dog's bitten me.
Stop biting your nails!
She bit into the apple.

bitter   not sweet

blackberry   a small, soft, black berry that grows on bushes

blackbird   a bird often seen in gardens. The male is black with a yellow beak, but the female is brown.

blackbirds

blackboard   a piece of black or dark green wood that you can write on with chalk

blacksmith   someone whose job is to make horseshoes and other things out of iron

blade   **1** the flat, sharp part of a knife or sword
2 something shaped like a blade
a blade of grass

blame   to say that it is because of a certain person or thing that something bad has happened
He blamed his broken pen for his untidy writing.

blancmange   (*say* bla-monj)
a kind of jelly made from sugar, milk, and flour

blank   with nothing written or drawn on it
a blank page

blanket   a thick cover used on a bed

blast   **1** sudden, rushing wind or air
A blast of cold air came through the open door.
2 to blow up
The miners used explosives to blast away the rocks.

blaze   to burn brightly
The fire was blazing in the grate.

blazer   a kind of jacket. A blazer usually has a badge on its top pocket.

bleach   to make something white

bleak   cold, miserable, and windy
a bleak day

bleat   to make the sound sheep make

bleed   to lose blood
His nose bled for ten minutes.

blend   to mix together

bless   to ask God to look after someone and make them happy
God bless you.

blew   see **blow**

blind   **1** not able to see
2 a screen that you pull down to cover a window

blink   to close your eyes and open them again very quickly

blister   a small swelling on the skin. It has liquid inside and hurts when you touch it.

blizzard   a storm with a lot of snow and wind

block   **1** a thick piece of something solid like wood or stone
2 to be in the way so that something cannot get through

blond, blonde   with fair hair

blood   a red liquid that moves round inside the body

bloom   to be in flower
Roses bloom in summer.

blossom   flowers on a tree

blot   a spot of ink spilt on something

blotting-paper   thick paper that dries ink quickly

blouse   a piece of clothing worn on the top half of the body by women and girls

blow   **1** to make air come out of the mouth
She blew out the candles and cut the cake.
2 to move along with the wind
Tiles were blown off the roof.

bluebell   a wild plant with flowers like tiny blue bells
(See picture on p. 218)

blunder   **1** to make a big mistake
2 to move about very clumsily

blunt   not sharp
a blunt knife

blur   to make something look less clear. Smudged writing is blurred.

blush   to go red in the face because you feel shy or guilty

boar   a wild pig

board   **1** a long piece of thin wood
2 stiff cardboard
3 to get on an aeroplane, bus, ship, or train

boast   to talk in a way that shows you are much too proud of yourself and what you can do
He boasted about his football skills.

boat   something that floats and has room in it for taking people or things over water

boats

body   **1** all of a person or animal that can be seen or touched
a dead body
2 all of a person except his legs, arms, and head

bodyguard   a person, or persons, whose job is to protect someone

bog   a piece of ground so wet and soft that your feet sink into it

boil   **1** to heat liquid until it bubbles
2 to cook something in hot, bubbling water
3 a big, painful spot on the skin

boiler   a large container in which water is heated

bold   brave and not afraid

bolt   **1** to rush off
The frightened horse bolted.
2 to swallow food quickly without chewing it
3 a kind of sliding fastener used on doors
He fastened the bolt on the back door.
4 a thick metal pin like a screw
a nut and bolt

bomb   a weapon that blows up and does a lot of damage

bone   any of the separate parts of a skeleton

bonfire   a large fire built in the open air

bonnet   **1** a hat that is tied under the chin
2 the part of a car that covers the engine

book   **1** sheets of paper fastened together and fixed to a cover
2 to arrange for a seat to be kept for you. You can book seats on coaches and trains and also at theatres and cinemas.

bookcase   a piece of furniture made for holding books

boom   to make a loud, deep sound
The guns boomed away in the distance.

boomerang   a curved stick that comes back to the person who throws it

boot   **1** a kind of shoe that also covers the ankle
2 the part of a car for carrying luggage

border   **1** the narrow part along the edge of something
a border of flowers
2 the line where two countries meet
She needed her passport to cross the border.

bore   **1** to make someone tired by being dull
a boring film
2 to make a hole with a tool
3 see **bear**

born, borne   see **bear**

borrow   to get the use of something for a short time and agree to give it back

boss   the person who is in charge

both   the two of them
He took both of the cakes.

bother   **1** to worry or annoy someone
Is the loud music bothering you?
2 to take trouble over doing something
He never bothers to tidy his room.

bottle   a glass container for liquids that is narrow at the top
a milk bottle

bottom   **1** the lowest part of anything
2 the part of the body that you sit on

bough   (*rhymes with* cow)
a large branch

bought   see **buy**

boulder   a large, smooth rock

bounce   to spring back after hitting something hard

bound   **1** to leap
2 see **bind**

boundary   a line marking the edge of some land

bouquet   (*say* boo-kay)
a bunch of flowers

bow[1]   (*rhymes with* go)
1 a strip of bent wood with string joining each end. It is used for shooting arrows.
2 a wooden rod with strong hairs stretched along it and joining each end, for playing the violin
3 a knot with loops
a bow in her hair

bow[2]   (*rhymes with* cow)
to bend forwards to show respect
He bowed to the Queen.

bowl   **1** a round, open container for liquid or food
2 to throw a ball to the batsman

box **1** a container with a lid
a cardboard box
2 to fight with the fists

boy a male child or teenager

brace a piece of wire worn across teeth to straighten them

bracelet beads, a chain, or a ring worn round the arm

bracelets

braces a pair of straps worn to keep up trousers

bracket **1** a piece of metal fixed to a wall to support something
The shelf rests on two brackets.
2 one of a pair of marks like these ( )

brag to talk in a way that shows you are much too proud of yourself and what you can do
She bragged that she was the best runner in the class.

brain the part inside the top of the head that controls the body. It also makes people able to think and remember.

brake the part of a car or bicycle that makes it slow down or stop

bramble a blackberry bush or a prickly bush like it

branch a part that sticks out from the trunk of a tree

brand **1** a mark to show the maker or owner
The farmer put a brand of blue dye on the sheep's back.
2 a certain kind of goods
a new brand of tea

brass a yellow metal made by mixing copper with zinc

brave **1** ready and able to bear pain or danger
2 a male American Indian

bravery the ability to be brave

bray to make the harsh sound a donkey makes

bread a food made by baking dough in loaves

breadth the measurement or distance across something

break **1** to snap, smash, or crack
The cup broke when I dropped it.
2 to fail to keep a law or promise
He's broken the rules.
3 a short rest from work
take a break

breakfast the first meal of the day

breath the air that a person breathes

breathe to take air into your lungs through your nose or mouth and send it out again
She was breathing quickly after the race.

breed to keep animals in order to get young ones from them
Last year he bred rabbits.

breeze a gentle wind

brick a small, oblong block used in building

bride a woman on the day she gets married

bridegroom a man on the day he gets married

bridesmaid a girl or woman who walks behind the bride at her wedding

bridge something built to go over a river, railway, or road

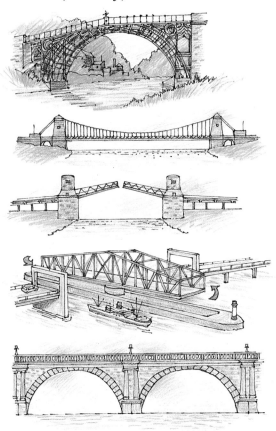

bridges

bridle the parts of a harness used for controlling a horse

brief short
a brief talk

brigade an organized group of people in uniform
the fire brigade

bright **1** shining
a bright star
2 intelligent
a bright boy
3 cheerful
a bright smile

brilliant very bright
brilliant light
a brilliant scientist

brim **1** the edge round the top of a container
a cup filled to the brim
2 the part of a hat that sticks out round the edge

bring **1** to carry here
Bring your book.
2 to lead here
Yesterday he brought his friend.

brink the edge of a dangerous place
He trembled on the brink of the precipice.

brisk quick and lively

bristle a short, stiff hair like the hairs on a brush

brittle likely to break or snap

broad measuring a lot from side to side
a broad river

broadcast a television or radio programme

broke, broken see **break**

bronze a brown metal made by mixing copper and tin

brooch (*rhymes with* coach)
a piece of jewellery worn pinned to clothing

brook a small stream

broom a sweeping brush with a long handle

broth a thin soup made from meat and vegetables

25

brother   a man or boy who has the same parents as another person

brought   see **bring**

brow   **1** the forehead
He wiped the sweat from his brow.
2 the top of a hill
When they reached the brow of the hill they rested.

Brownie   a junior Guide

bruise   a coloured mark that comes on the skin when it has been hit hard

brush   a tool with short, stiff hairs. Brushes are used for making hair tidy, cleaning, sweeping, scrubbing, and painting.

bubble   **1** a small ball of air inside liquid
2 to be full of bubbles

buck   **1** a male deer, hare, or rabbit
2 to leap like a horse about to throw someone off its back

bucket   a container with a handle but no lid, used for carrying liquid

buckle   a kind of fastening used on belts or straps

bud   a flower or leaf before it has opened

Buddhism   the religion following the teachings of Buddha

budge   to move slightly

budgerigar   a small, brightly coloured bird often kept as a pet

buffalo   a kind of wild ox. Buffaloes are found in Africa, India, and North America.

buffet   (*say* buffay)
a place where you can get drinks and snacks

bugle   a small, brass musical instrument that you blow into

build   to make something by putting things carefully on top of one another
Last autumn we built a huge bonfire.

building   something that has been built. Houses, schools, theatres, shops, and churches are all buildings

built   see **build**

bulb   **1** the part of a lamp that gives light
2 something that looks like an onion and is planted in soil. Daffodils, tulips, and some other flowers grow from bulbs.

bulge   to swell out
His pockets were bulging with conkers.

bulk   a large amount

bull   a male ox, elephant, or whale

bulldozer   a heavy machine for clearing land

bullet   a small lump of metal made to be fired from a gun

bullock   a young, male ox

bully   someone who attacks or threatens a weaker person

bulrush   a tall plant that grows near water

bulrushes

bump   **1** to knock against something by accident
The giant bumped his head on the ceiling.
2 a swelling
a painful bump on the head

bumper   a bar along the front or back of a car. It protects the car if it hits something.

bunch   a group of things joined or tied together

bundle   a group of things tied together
a bundle of sticks

bungalow   a house without any upstairs rooms

bunk   a bed that has another bed above or below it

buoy   (*say* boy)
a thing in the sea to warn ships about danger

burden   something that has to be carried

burglar   someone who gets into a building to steal things

burial   (*say* berrial)
the burying of a dead person

burn   **1** to hurt or damage something with fire or heat
2 to be on fire

burrow   a hole in the ground that an animal lives in
Rabbits live in burrows.

burst   to break open suddenly because there is too much inside

bury   to put something or someone in a hole in the ground and cover it over

bush   a plant that looks like a small tree

business   (*say* biznis)
1 a person's work
My father's business is selling cars.
2 a shop or firm or industry

bustle   to hurry in a busy or fussy way

busy   **1** doing things all the time
2 full of activity
a busy street

butcher   someone whose job is to cut up meat and sell it

butter   a yellow food made from cream. It is spread on bread.

buttercup   a wild flower with shiny yellow petals (See picture on p. 218)

butterfly   an insect with large white or coloured wings

butterflies

butterscotch   hard toffee made from sugar and butter

button a fastener sewn on clothes. It fits into a hole or loop.

buy to get something by giving money for it
I bought this bike from him yesterday.

buzz to make the sound a bee makes

C c

cab 1 the part of a lorry, bus, or train where the driver sits
2 a taxi

cabbage a vegetable with a lot of green leaves

cabin 1 a room in a ship or aeroplane (See picture on p. 215)
2 a small hut
a log cabin

cabinet a kind of cupboard with drawers

cable strong, thick wire or rope

cackle to laugh and make the sound a hen makes

cactus a plant with a thick green stem and thick green branches, covered in prickles. Cacti grow in hot, dry places and do not need much water. (See picture on p. 218)

café (*say* kaffay)
a place where you can buy a drink, a snack, or a meal

cafeteria a kind of café where you fetch your own food from the counter

cage a box with bars across it for keeping animals in

cake a food made with flour, butter, eggs, and sugar

calamity something very bad that happens suddenly

calculator a machine that can do sums

calendar a list showing all the days, weeks, and months in a year

calf 1 a young cow, elephant, or whale
two calves
2 the back part of the leg between the knee and the ankle

caliper a pair of metal bars worn to support a weak leg

call 1 to speak loudly
2 to give a name to someone or something
3 to tell someone to come to you
The mother called the children.

calm (*say* karm)
1 still
a calm sea
2 not noisy or excited

calves more than one **calf**

came see **come**

camel a big animal with one or two humps on its back. Camels are used instead of horses in deserts, because they can travel for a long time without eating or drinking.

camels

camera a machine for taking photographs (See picture on p. 222)

camouflage
to hide something by making it look like other things that are near it. Most wild animals are camouflaged by their colour or shape, when they are not moving.

camp **1** a group of tents or huts where people live for a short time
2 *to go camping* to have a holiday living in a tent

can **1** to be able to
I can swim – he can't.
He could read before he started school. I couldn't.
2 a tin
a can of coke

canal a kind of river made by people, so that boats can go straight from one place to another

canary a small yellow bird that sings

cancer a serious disease in which lumps grow in the body

candle a stick of wax with string through the centre. It gives light as it burns.

candlestick something to hold a candle

cane **1** the hard stem of some plants
2 a long, thin stick

cannon a big gun that fires heavy metal balls

canoe (*say* ca-<u>noo</u>)
a light, narrow boat that you move by using a paddle (See picture on p. 215)

canteen a kind of café that sells food to people in a school, factory, or office

canter one of the ways a horse can move. It is faster than a trot but slower than a gallop.

canvas strong material for making things like tents

capable able to do something
You're capable of better work.

capacity the largest amount a container can hold
The capacity of a milk bottle is one pint.

cape a short cloak

capital **1** the most important city in a country
London is the capital of England.
2 one of the big letters put at the beginning of names and sentences. A, B, C, D, and so on are **capital letters**.

capsule **1** something that looks like a sweet, but has medicine inside. It has to be swallowed whole.
2 a separate part at the front of a spaceship. It can move on its own, away from the main part.

capsule 2

captain **1** an officer in the army or navy
2 someone who is in charge of a team

captive a person or animal that has been captured

capture 1 to take prisoner
2 to get something by fighting for it

caramel soft toffee

caravan a house on wheels that can be pulled by a car or truck from place to place

carburettor the part of an engine that mixes the petrol with air

card 1 thick, stiff paper
2 a piece of card with a picture and a message on it. You send cards to people at special times like Christmas.
3 one of a set of small pieces of card with numbers or pictures on them, used in games (See picture on p. 222)

cardboard very thick, strong paper

cardigan a kind of knitted jacket

care 1 worry or trouble
2 *to take care of* to look after
3 *to care for* to look after
4 *to care about* to be very interested in something

careful making sure that you do things safely and well
a careful driver

careless not careful

caretaker someone whose job is to look after a building

cargo things taken by ship or aeroplane from one place to another
cargoes of fruit

carnation a garden plant with white, pink, or red flowers that smells very sweet (See picture on p. 218)

carnival a colourful procession with people wearing fancy dress

carol a happy song sung at Christmas

carpenter someone whose job is to make things out of wood

carpet a thick cover for the floor

carriage 1 one of the separate parts of a train where passengers sit
2 a vehicle on wheels pulled by horses

carriage 2

carrot an orange vegetable shaped like a cone

carry to take people, animals, or things from one place to another
We carried the shopping bags all the way home.

cart a kind of box on wheels. It is pulled by a horse or pushed by a person.

carton   a light container made of cardboard or plastic

cartoon   **1** a film that uses drawings instead of actors
a Mickey Mouse cartoon
2 a drawing that tells a joke

cartridge   a case or tube holding film, tape or ink

carve   **1** to cut wood or stone to make a picture or a shape
2 to cut off slices of meat

cascade   a waterfall

case   **1** a container
a pencil case
2 a suitcase

cash   coins or paper money

cassette   a small, closed container with a reel of tape inside it for recording or playing sounds

cast   **1** a shape made by pouring liquid metal or plaster into a mould
2 all the actors in a play
3 to throw
He cast his net into the sea to catch fish.

castaway   someone who has been shipwrecked

castle   a large, strong house with very thick, stone walls. Castles were built long ago to keep the people inside them safe from their enemies.
Windsor Castle

catalogue   a complete list

catapult   a piece of elastic joined to a stick shaped like a Y for shooting small stones

catch   **1** to capture
2 to get hold of something
3 to get an illness
I caught a cold last week.

caterpillar   a long, creeping creature that will turn into a butterfly or moth

caterpillars

cathedral   a big, important church
Durham Cathedral

catkin   one of the tiny flowers that hang down in clusters on some trees

cattle   cows and bulls kept by a farmer

caught   see **catch**

cauldron   a large pot used for cooking
a witch's cauldron

cauliflower   a vegetable with a thick white stalk covered in small, hard, white flowers

cause   to make something happen
The wind caused the door to slam.

cautious   only doing what is safe
a cautious man

cavalry   a group of men trained to fight while riding horses

cave   a big hole under the ground or inside a mountain

cavern   a large cave

cease   to stop doing something

ceiling   the surface above you in a room
Stand on a ladder to paint the ceiling.

celebrate   to do special things to show you are very happy about something. Every year people celebrate Christmas.

celebration   a party for something special

celery   a vegetable with white stalks that can be eaten raw

cell   **1** one of the small rooms where prisoners are kept in a prison
2 the tiniest part of a living thing

cellar   a room underneath a building. Cellars are used for storing things.

Celsius   a way of measuring temperature that gives 0 degrees for freezing water and 100 degrees for boiling water

cement   a mixture of clay and lime used in building to stick things together

cemetery   a place where dead people are buried

centigrade   an older name for Celsius

centimetre   a measure for length
My ruler is 30 centimetres long.

centipede   a long, creeping creature with a lot of tiny legs

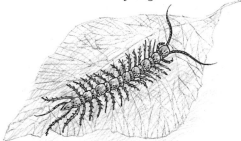

centre   the middle of something

century   a hundred years

cereal   **1** any plant grown by farmers for its seed
2 a food made from the seed of cereal plants and eaten at breakfast with milk

ceremony   (*say* serimony) something important and serious that is done in front of other people
a marriage ceremony

certain   **1** sure
Are you certain?
2 one in particular
a certain person

certificate   a piece of paper that says you have done something special

chaffinch   a small bird. Its front is red and it has white marks on its wings.

chain   a line made of metal rings fastened together

chair   a seat for one person

chalet   (*say* shallay) a small, wooden house with a large roof

chalk   **1** a kind of soft white rock
2 a soft white stick used for writing on blackboards

a b c d e f g h i j k l m n o p q r s t u v w x y z

challenge to ask someone to try to do better than you at something

champion **1** someone who is the best in their sport
2 an animal or plant that wins a competition

championship a competition to decide on the champion

chance **1** a time when you can do something that you cannot do at other times
This is your last chance.
2 the way things happen that have not been planned
I saw him by chance on the bus.

change **1** to make or become different
Tadpoles change into frogs.
2 to give something and get something in return
They changed places with each other.
3 the money that you get back when you give more money than is needed to pay for something
The shop-assistant gave him the change.

channel **1** a narrow sea
the English Channel
2 a groove in the ground that water moves along
3 the name given to a television station
Which channel shall we watch?

chapel a kind of church

chapter a part of a book

character **1** someone in a story
2 the sort of person you are

charge **1** to ask a certain price
They charge 70p for a school dinner.
2 to rush at something to attack it
3 *in charge* with the job of telling other people what they should do or how they should do it

chariot a kind of cart with two wheels, pulled by horses. Chariots were used long ago for fighting and racing.

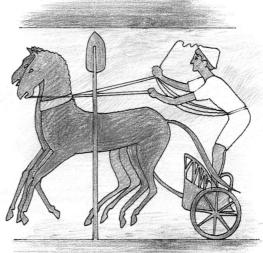

charity any group of people who raise money to help others
Which charities does your school support?

charm **1** a magic spell
2 a small ornament worn to bring good luck
3 to cast a spell over someone or something

chart **1** a big map
2 a large sheet of paper with information on it

chase to run after and try to catch a person or animal

chat to talk in a friendly way about things that are not important

chatter **1** to talk a lot or very quickly
2 to make a rattling noise
His teeth chattered with fear.

chauffeur (*say* show-fur) someone whose job is to drive another person's car for them

cheap costing less than usual

cheat **1** to make another person believe what is not true so that you can get something from them
2 to try to do well in a test or game, by breaking the rules

check **1** to go over something to make sure it is correct
2 a pattern of squares

check-out the place in a shop where you pay for what you have bought

cheek **1** the side of the face below the eye
2 rude behaviour or speech

cheer to shout to show you are pleased or that you want your team to win

cheerful looking or sounding happy
a cheerful face

cheese food made by stirring milk until it becomes solid

chemist someone whose job is to make or sell medicines

cherry a small, round, red or black fruit with a stone in it

cheque (*say* check)
a special form that a person can sign and use instead of money to pay for something

chest **1** a big, strong box
2 the front part of the body between the neck and the waist

chestnut **1** a kind of tree
2 the shiny brown nut that grows on a chestnut tree

chew **1** to keep biting food while you eat it
2 a kind of sweet

chicken a young bird kept for its meat and eggs

chicken-pox an illness that gives you red spots that itch

chief **1** the most important
2 the person in charge

child **1** a young boy or girl
2 a son or daughter
two children

chill **1** a bad cold that makes you feel hot and dizzy
2 to make something cold

chime to make a tune like church bells

chimney a tall pipe inside the wall of a house to take away the smoke from a fire

chimpanzee an African animal like a large monkey with long arms and no tail

chin the part of the face that is under the mouth

china cups, saucers, and plates made of very thin, delicate pottery

chip **1** a small piece of potato that is fried
2 to break or knock small pieces off something
a chipped vase
3 a small electronic part in a computer

chisel a tool with a short, sharp edge, for cutting stone or wood

chocolate sweet food made from cocoa and sugar

choice 1 choosing
a choice of three different flavours of ice-cream
2 what you have chosen

choir (*say* kwire)
a group of people who sing together

choke 1 to find it hard to get your breath because of something in your throat
The smoke made him choke.
2 to block up something
The pond was choked with weeds.

choose to take one thing instead of another, because you want to
Which car have you chosen?
Last time you chose to go to the zoo.

chop 1 to cut something by hitting it hard with a sharp tool
2 a small, thick slice of pork or lamb

chopsticks a pair of thin sticks held in one hand that Chinese and Japanese people use instead of a knife and fork

chorus (*say* ko-russ)
the words repeated after every verse in a poem or song

chose, chosen see **choose**

christen to give a baby its name in church and welcome it into God's family
The minister christened the baby yesterday.

Christian someone who believes in Jesus Christ

Christmas the 25th December when Jesus Christ's birthday is celebrated

chrome, chromium (*say* krome, krome-ium)
a bright, shiny metal that looks like silver

chrysalis (*say* kriss-a-liss)
the cover a caterpillar makes round itself before it changes into a butterfly or moth

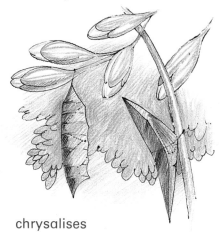

chrysalises

chrysanthemum an autumn flower with a lot of petals that grows in gardens

chuckle to laugh to yourself

chunk a thick lump
a chunk of cheese

church a building where people worship God

churn 1 a large container for milk
2 a machine for turning milk into butter

cigar tobacco leaves that are rolled and then smoked

cigarette a thin tube of paper with tobacco inside it for smoking

cinders the grey pieces left when coal has finished burning

cinema a place where people go to see films

circle 1 the shape of a coin or wheel. The edge of a circle is always the same distance from the centre. (See the list of shapes on p. 223) 2 the curved line round the edge of a circle

circular like a circle

circus a show held in a big tent or building with animals, acrobats, and clowns

city a big town

claim to ask for something that belongs to you
She claimed her lost property.

clang to make the loud, ringing sound a heavy metal door makes when you shut it

clank to make the hard sound that heavy metal chains make when they bang against each other

clap to make a noise by hitting the palm of one hand with the palm of the other

clash 1 to make the sound cymbals make
2 to disagree with someone

clasp to hold tightly

class a group of pupils who learn things together

clatter to make the rattling sound a horse's hooves make on the road

claw one of the hard, sharp nails that some animals have on their feet

clay a sticky kind of earth used for making things, because it keeps its shape and goes hard

clean 1 not dirty
a clean face
2 to make something clean
Clean your teeth.

clear 1 easy to understand, see, or hear
a clear photograph, a clear voice
2 free from things you do not want
a clear road, a clear day
3 to make something clear
Please clear the table.

clench to close your teeth, fingers, or fist tightly to show that you are determined to do something

clerk (*rhymes with* park)
someone who sorts out papers and writes letters in an office

clever able to learn and understand things easily

click the short, sharp sound an electric light switch makes

cliff a steep rock close to the sea

climate the sort of weather that a place usually gets at different times of the year

climb   to go up or down something high

cling   to hold tightly on to someone or something
The child was afraid and clung to its mother.

clinic   **1** a kind of hospital
2 a kind of surgery where doctors work together

clip   **1** to cut something with scissors or a tool like scissors
He clipped the hedge.
2 a fastener for keeping things together or in place
a paper clip

cloak   a very loose coat without sleeves

cloakroom   the room where you hang your coat

clock   a machine that shows you what time it is

clocks

clockwise   the direction in which a clock's hands move

clockwork   able to work when it is wound up like a clock. Clockwork toys can move by themselves.

close¹   (*rhymes with* dose)
1 very near
close to the fire
2 careful
a close look
3 a street closed at one end

close²   (*rhymes with* doze)
1 to shut
All the shops are closing early today.
2 to end
The village shop is closing down.

cloth   **1** material for making things like clothes and curtains
2 a piece of cloth for cleaning or covering something

clothes, clothing   things worn to cover the body

cloud   **1** something white, grey, or black that floats in the sky. Clouds are made of drops of water that often fall as rain.
2 dust or smoke that looks like a cloud

clout   to hit hard with your hand

clover   a wild flower. Each of its leaves is like three small leaves joined together.

clown   someone in a circus who wears funny clothes and make-up and makes people laugh

club   **1** a group of people who meet together because they are interested in the same thing
2 a thick stick used as a weapon
3 a black clover leaf printed on some playing-cards (See picture on p. 222)
the ace of clubs

cluck   to make a noise like a hen

clue   something that helps you to find the answer to a puzzle

clump   a group of trees or plants growing close together

clumsy   likely to knock things over or drop things, because you move badly

clung   see **cling**

cluster   **1** a group of things growing together
a cluster of berries
2 a group of people, animals, or things gathered round something
The horses clustered round the pond.

clutch   **1** to snatch at something
2 to hold tightly
3 part of a car's mechanical system

coach   **1** a bus that takes people on long journeys
2 one of the separate parts of a train, where passengers sit
3 someone who trains people in a sport

coach 1

coal   hard, black rock that is burned to make heat

coarse   not delicate or smooth. Sacks are made of coarse material.

coast   the edge of land next to the sea

coat   something with long sleeves that people put on top of other clothes when they go out

cobbler   someone whose job is to mend shoes

cobweb   a thin, sticky net spun by a spider to trap insects

cockerel   a young, male bird kept with hens

cocoa   a brown powder used to make a hot drink that tastes of chocolate

coconut   a big, round, hard seed that grows on palm trees. It has a sweet white food and liquid inside.

coconuts

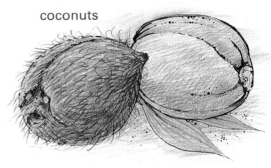

cod   a large sea fish that can be eaten   (See picture on p. 220)

code   **1** a set of signs or letters for sending messages secretly or quickly
2 a set of rules
the Highway Code

coffee   a hot drink. It is made from roasted beans crushed into a brown powder.

coffin   the long box in which a dead person is put

coil   to wind rope or wire into rings

coin   a piece of metal money

coke   **1** black stuff that is made from coal and can be burnt instead of coal
2 a brown, fizzy drink

cold   **1** like ice or snow feels
2 an illness that makes you sneeze and blow your nose a lot

collage
a picture made from small pieces of paper and material

collapse   **1** to fall to pieces
The shed collapsed in the strong wind.
2 to fall down because you are ill
The old lady collapsed and was taken to hospital.

collar　**1** the part that goes round the neck of clothes such as shirts and jackets
2 a band put round the neck of a dog or cat

collect　**1** to bring things together from different places
I collect foreign coins.
2 to go and get someone or something
She collected the children from school.

collection　**1** a set of things that have been collected
a stamp collection
2 money collected from many people for a special reason

collector　someone who collects things as a hobby or as a job

college　**1** a kind of school
2 a place where people can carry on learning about something when they are too old for school

collide　to hit someone or something by accident

collie　a long-haired sheep dog
(See picture on p. 220)

colliery　a coal mine

collision　a crash between two moving things

colon　a mark like this :

colour　**1** red, blue, and green are colours
(See the list of colours p. 223.)
2 to use paint or crayon on something

colt　a young, male horse

column　**1** things on a list each below the other
2 a thick stone post that supports something or decorates a building
Nelson's Column

comb　**1** a strip of plastic, wood, or metal with a row of thin parts like teeth, for making hair tidy
2 to search a place very carefully
Police combed the area for the lost child.

combine　to join or mix together

combine harvester　a machine that cuts down corn and gets the seed out of it

come　**1** to move here
I came as soon as I could.
2 to arrive
Has the letter come yet?

comedian　someone who entertains people by making them laugh

comedy　a funny play

comfortable　pleasant to be in, to sit on, or to wear
a comfortable chair

comic　**1** funny
2 a paper with stories told in pictures

comma　a mark like this ,

command　**1** to tell someone to do something
The captain was in command.
2 to be in charge of something

common **1** usual
a common illness
2 a piece of land that anyone can use

commotion a lot of noise
There was a great commotion when a dog ran into the school assembly.

communication **1** a message
2 a way of sending or getting a message

community the people living in one place

companion a friend who is with you

company **1** having an animal or another person with you so that you are not lonely
The cat kept her company.
2 a group of people who do things together
a company of actors

compare to try to see how like each other some things are

compass an instrument that always shows where north is. A compass helps you to find your way when you are lost.

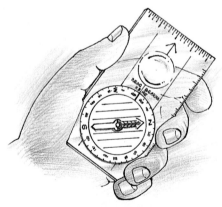

compasses an instrument for drawing circles
a pair of compasses

compete to take part in a race or competition

competition a kind of test or game with a prize for the person who wins

complain to say that you are not pleased about something

complete **1** whole, with nothing missing
The jigsaw is complete – all the pieces are there.
2 to come to the end of something

complicated **1** with a lot of different parts
a complicated machine
2 difficult
a complicated sum

compliment words that praise the person you are speaking or writing to
She was paid a compliment when they said her dancing was excellent.

composer someone who writes music

composition a story you have made up and written down

computer a machine which stores information on tape or disk, organizes it and then produces it when someone needs it

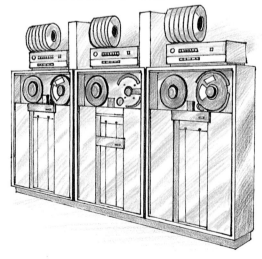

conceal   to hide
The money was concealed under the floor.

conceited   too proud of yourself and what you can do

concentrate   to think hard about one thing

concern   **1** to be important or interesting to someone or something
The information about the school trip concerned everyone.
2 *concerned*   worried

concert   an entertainment with music

concrete   a mixture of cement and sand used for making buildings, paths, and bridges

condense   to make something smaller

condition   the state something is in
The road surface is in poor condition.

conductor   **1** someone who sells tickets on a bus and looks after the passengers
This bus doesn't have a conductor; you have to pay the driver.
2 someone who stands facing a band, choir, or orchestra and keeps everyone playing together

cone   **1** the shape of a witch's hat or an ice-cream cornet
(See the list of shapes on p. 223.)
2 a case for seeds on evergreen trees
a fir cone

confess   to say that you have done something wrong
He confessed to breaking the window.

confetti   tiny pieces of coloured paper that are thrown over a bride and bridegroom

confident   **1** brave and not afraid
a confident swimmer
2 sure about something
She was confident she knew the way.

confuse   to mix up
He always confuses the names of the twins.

congratulate   to tell someone how pleased you are about something special that has happened to them

conjuror   someone who entertains people by doing tricks that look like magic

conker   the hard, shiny brown nut that grows on a horse-chestnut tree

connect   to join together
She connected the hose to the tap.

conquer   to beat in a battle or war

conscious   (*say* kon-shuss)
awake and able to understand what is happening around you
After the operation he slowly became conscious.

conservation   taking good care of the world's air, water, plants, and animals

consider   to think carefully about something

considerable   large
a considerable amount of money

considerate   kind and thoughtful in the way you behave towards other people

consonant   any letter of the alphabet except a e i o u and sometimes y

constable   an ordinary policeman or policewoman

constellation   a group of stars that form pictures or patterns in the sky

construct   to build

contain   to have something inside
The box contained toys.

container   anything that you can put other things into. Buckets, cups, bags, boxes, and jars are all containers.

contented   happy with what you have

contents   what is inside a container or a book
Be careful – the contents of this box are very fragile.

contest   a competition

continent   one of the seven very large areas of land in the world (See list of continents on p. 224)

continue   to go on doing something
They continued the game after lunch.

contradict   to say that someone is saying something that is not true
The teacher contradicted the child who said that the earth was flat.

control   to be in charge of something and be able to make it do what you want

convenient   easy to get at or use

convent   a place where nuns live and work together

conversation   talking and listening to another person

convict   a criminal who is in prison

convince   to make someone believe something
He convinced her that ghosts were not real.

cook   **1** to get food ready to eat by heating it
2 someone whose job is to cook

cookery   cooking food

cool   not warm
a cool drink

copper   a shiny brown or red metal used for making pipes and coins

copy   **1** to write down or draw what is already written down or drawn
She copied the poem in her best writing.
2 to do exactly the same as someone else
She always copies what I wear.

coral a kind of rock made in the sea from the bodies of tiny creatures. Coral can be many colours.

cord thin rope

core the part in the middle of something
an apple core

corgi a kind of light brown dog with very short legs and pointed ears (See picture on p. 220)

cork The bark of a special kind of oak tree. It is put into the top of a bottle to close it.

corkscrew a tool for getting corks out of bottles

corn grain

corner the point where two edges or streets meet

cornet a wafer shaped like a cone, for holding ice-cream

cornflakes a kind of food made from corn, eaten with milk at breakfast

coronation the time when someone is crowned as king or queen

corpse a dead body

correct without any mistakes

corridor a long, narrow passage inside a big building or train. It has doors along it and people go down it to get from one room to another.

cost to have a certain price
The bike cost £100.

costume 1 clothes worn on the stage
2 clothes like ones worn long ago

cosy warm and comfortable

cottage a small house in the country

cotton 1 thread for sewing
2 a light cloth made from a plant that grows in hot countries
a cool cotton dress

cotton wool soft, white, fluffy, cotton stuff. Cotton wool is used in looking after babies and injured people and in packing delicate things.

couch a settee or sofa

cough to make a sudden, loud noise to get rid of something in your throat. Smoke and bad colds make people cough.

could see **can**

council a group of people chosen to plan and decide what should be done in a place
a City Council

count 1 to say the numbers in order
2 to use numbers to find out how many people or things there are in a place

counter 1 the long table where you are served in a shop, cafeteria, or bank
2 a small, round, flat piece of plastic used for playing some games

country 1 a land with its own people and laws. England, Australia, and China are all countries.
2 the countryside

countryside land with farms and villages, away from towns

county one of the large areas Britain and Ireland are divided into

couple two
a couple of sweets

coupon a kind of ticket that you can change for a free gift. Some coupons make you able to buy things for less money than usual.

courage the ability to be brave

course 1 the direction something takes
a ship's course
2 a piece of ground where some kinds of sport take place
3 a series of lessons
a swimming course

court 1 a piece of ground marked out for a game like netball or tennis
2 the place where a king or queen is living and the people who are with them
3 the place where people decide whether someone is guilty of breaking the law

cousin the child of your aunt or uncle

cover 1 to put one thing over or round another thing
2 something used for covering things

coward someone who is afraid when they ought to be brave

cowboy a man who rides round looking after the cattle on large farms in America

cowslip a yellow wild flower that grows in the spring
(See picture on p. 218)

crab an animal with a shell, claws, and ten legs that lives in or near the sea

crabs

crack 1 to make the sudden, sharp noise a dry twig makes when you snap it
2 a line on the surface of something where it has been partly broken. Cracks can come in walls, ceilings, cups, and plates.

cracker 1 a paper tube with a toy and paper hat inside. It bangs when two people pull it apart.
Christmas crackers
2 a thin biscuit that is not sweet

crackle to make the cracking sounds burning wood makes

cradle a baby's bed

craftsman someone who is very good at doing difficult work with their hands

crafty clever at planning things so that you get your own way

crane 1 a machine on wheels for lifting very heavy things
2 a large bird with very long legs

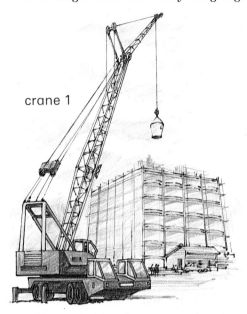
crane 1

crash 1 the loud noise made when something heavy is dropped and smashed
2 to hit something with a loud noise
The car crashed into a tree.

crate a container for carrying bottles or other things that break easily

crawl 1 to move on your hands and knees
2 to move slowly
The car crawled along in the fog.
3 a way of swimming

crayon 1 a stick of coloured wax used for drawing
2 a coloured pencil

crazy likely to do strange or silly things

creak to make a loud, rough, squeaking noise. New shoes, doors that need oiling, and old wooden stairs creak.

cream 1 the thick part on the top of milk
2 the colour of cream
3 something that looks like cream and is put on the skin
hand-cream

crease to make a line in something by folding it

create to make something no one else has made or can make
The sculptor created a new statue.

creator someone who makes what no one else has made or can make

creature any animal

credit card a piece of plastic with your name and a number on it, which lets you buy goods that you need now and pay for them later

creek a small stream

creep 1 to move along, keeping close to the ground
2 to move quietly or secretly
We crept away and nobody saw us.

crêpe paper (*say* krape paper) thin, coloured paper that you can stretch

crept see **creep**

crescent a street shaped like a curved line

cress a small, green plant that is eaten raw

crew a group of people who work together on a boat or aeroplane

cricket 1 a game played in a field by two teams with a ball, two bats, and two wickets
2 an insect that makes a shrill sound

cried see **cry**

crime an activity such as stealing which is against the law

criminal   someone who has done something bad that is against the law

crimson   a deep red colour

crinkle   to make small lines in skin or paper by creasing it

cripple   someone whose legs or arms are hurt so that they cannot use them properly

crisp   **1** very dry so that it breaks easily
2 firm and fresh
a very crisp apple
3 a very thin, dry slice of fried potato   *a packet of crisps*

criss-cross   with lines that cross each other

croak   to make the hoarse sound a frog makes

crocodile   a large reptile that lives in rivers in some hot countries. It has short legs, a long body, and sharp teeth.

crocus   a small white, yellow, or purple spring flower
(See picture on p. 218)

crook   **1** someone who cheats or robs people
2 a shepherd's stick with a curved top

crooked   not straight

crop   **1** plants grown on a farm for food
2 to bite off the tops of plants. Sheep crop grass.

cross   **1** to move across something
2 a mark like this + or ×
3 the shape of + or ×
4 angry

crouch   to lean forwards and bend your knees so that your bottom is almost touching the ground

crow   a big, black bird

crowd   a large number of people

crown   a big ring of silver or gold worn on the head by a king or queen

cruel   very unkind

cruise   to sail about without hurrying

crumb   a tiny bit of bread or cake

crumble   to break or fall into small pieces

crumple   to make something very creased
crumpled clothes

crunch   to eat with the noise you make when you eat crisps

crush to damage something by pressing it hard

crust the hard part round the outside of bread

crutch a wooden stick that a crippled person can lean on when they are walking. It fits under their arm.
a pair of crutches

cry **1** to let tears fall from your eyes
He was so upset that he cried.
2 to shout

crystal **1** a hard material like very bright glass
2 the shape of snowflakes

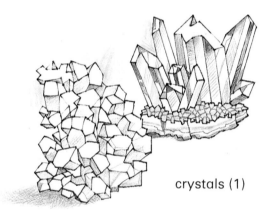

crystals (1)

cub a young bear, lion, tiger, or wolf

Cub Scout a junior Scout

cube the shape of dice or sugar lumps. Cubes have six square sides that are all the same size.
(See the list of shapes on p. 223.)

cuckoo a bird that lays its eggs in other birds' nests. The male cry sounds like *cuck-oo*.

cucumber a long, green vegetable eaten raw

cuddle to put your arms closely round a person or animal that you love

cuff the part joined to the end of a sleeve to fit round the wrist

cul-de-sac a street closed at one end
We live in a quiet cul-de-sac.

culprit the person who is guilty

cunning crafty

cupboard a piece of furniture or a space inside a wall. Cupboards have doors and usually some shelves.

cure to make well again

curiosity a wish to find out about things

curious **1** wanting to know about something
She was curious to know what her present would be.
2 unusual
a curious smell

curl **1** a piece of hair twisted into rings
2 *to curl up* to sit or lie comfortably with the body bent round itself

currant a small, black, dried grape

current water, air, or electricity moving in one direction

curry a cooked food with a spicy flavour

curtain a piece of cloth pulled in front of a window or stage to cover it

curtsy to put one foot behind the other and bend the knees. Women and girls curtsy.
She curtsied to the Queen.

curve a line that is bent smoothly like the letter C

cushion a cloth bag filled with soft material so that it is comfortable to sit on or rest against

custard a thick, sweet, yellow liquid poured over puddings

custom something that is usually done. It is a custom to give Christmas presents.

customer someone who uses a shop or a bank

cut **1** to use scissors or a knife to open, divide, or shape something
She's cutting out the picture.
I've cut up your meat for you.
2 an opening in the skin made by something sharp

cutlery knives, forks, and spoons

cycle to ride a bicycle

cygnet (*say* sig-nit) a young swan

cylinder the shape of a tin of soup or a toilet roll
(See the list of shapes on p. 223.)

cymbals a musical instrument that is two round pieces of metal that you bang together
a pair of cymbals

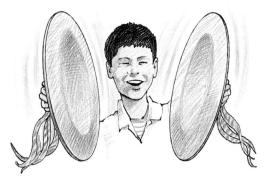

cypress a kind of tree. It has dark leaves that it keeps all through the year. (See picture on p. 219)

D d

dachshund a kind of dog with very short legs and a long body
(See picture on p. 220)

daffodil a yellow flower that grows from a bulb (See picture on p. 218)

daft silly

dagger a very short sword with two sharp edges

daily every day

dairy **1** a place where milk is made into butter and cheese
2 a shop that sells milk, cream, butter, and cheese

daisy a small flower with white petals and a yellow centre
(See picture on p. 218)

dale a valley

dam a wall built to hold water back. Some dams are built to stop floods happening.

damage to harm something
The rain damaged the wheat in the field.

damp a little wet
damp grass

damson a small, dark purple plum

dance to move about in time to music

dandelion a yellow wild flower with a thick stalk (See picture on p. 218)

danger 1 something that is dangerous
2 the chance of something dangerous happening
danger of fire

dangerous likely to kill or harm you
It's dangerous to play in the road.

dangle to hang loosely
He saw his scarf dangling from the branch.

dare 1 to be brave enough or rude enough to do something
I daren't dive in. How dare you!
2 to ask someone to show how brave they are
I dare you to climb that tree.

daring very brave

dark 1 without any light
a dark house
2 not light in colour
a dark green coat

darling someone who is loved very much

darn to sew over a hole in a garment to mend it

dart 1 to move very quickly and suddenly
2 something with a sharp point that you throw at a target

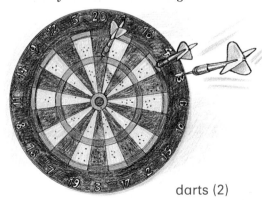

darts (2)

dash 1 to move very quickly
2 a mark like this –

data 1 facts or information
2 information that is being worked on by the program in a computer

date 1 the day, the month, and the year when something happens
2 a sweet, brown fruit that grows on a palm tree

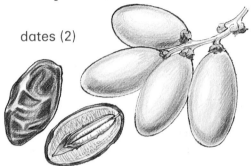

dates (2)

daughter a girl or woman who is someone's child

dawdle to walk too slowly
He was late for school because he was dawdling.

dawn the time of the day when the sun rises

day 1 the twenty four hours between midnight and the next midnight
2 the part of the day when it is light

dazed not able to think properly. People are often dazed after an accident.

dazzle to be so bright that it hurts your eyes to look
The sun was dazzling.

dead not alive

deaf not able to hear

deal 1 to give out
I dealt the cards last time.
2 *to deal with something* to do a job that needs doing
3 *a great deal* a lot

dealt   (*say* delt) see **deal**

dear   **1** loved. Dear is always used to begin letters, for example
Dear Uncle Tom . . .
2 costing a lot
butter is dear

death   the end of life

debt   something that you owe someone

decay   to go bad
Sugar makes teeth decay.

deceit   making someone believe something that is not true

deceive   to make someone believe something that is not true
They deceived the bus conductor, saying they had already paid.

decide   to make up your mind about something

decimal   **1** using tens
the decimal system
2 a way of writing fractions by putting numbers after a dot.
³⁄₁₀ is 0.3   ½ is 0.5

decision   what you have decided

deck   a floor on a ship or bus
(See picture on p. 215)

declare   to say something important that you want everyone to know
The mayor declared the fête open.

decorate   to make something look pretty

decrease   to make smaller or fewer
She decreased the number of stitches on her knitting-needles.

deed   something special that someone has done
a good deed

deep   going a long way down from the top
deep water, a deep hole

deer   a graceful animal that can move very quickly. Male deer have big horns like branches growing out of their heads.
two deer

deer

defeat   to beat someone in a game or battle

defend   to keep someone or something safe from attack
The soldiers defended the castle.

definite   fixed or certain
a definite date for the holiday

defy   to say or show that you will not obey

degree   a measurement for temperature. You can write it like this °, and so ten degrees is 10°.

delay   **1** to make someone or something late
2 to put off doing something until later

deliberate   done on purpose
a deliberate mistake

delicate   **1** soft and fine
delicate material
2 likely to get ill or damaged
a delicate child
delicate equipment

delicious   tasting or smelling very pleasant

delight   to please very much
The surprise gift delighted her.

deliver   **1** to bring things like milk or newspapers to someone's house **2** to set free

delivery   delivering something

demand   to ask for something that you think you ought to have
He demanded his money back.

demolish   to knock something down and break it up

demonstrate   to show
She's demonstrating how it works.

demonstration   a lot of people marching through the streets to show everyone what they think about something

dense   thick
a dense fog, a dense forest

dent   to make a hollow in something hard, by hitting it. Cars are often dented in accidents.

dentist   someone whose job is to look after teeth. Dentists can take out bad teeth or fill them.

deny   to say that something is not true
She denied breaking the cup.

depart   to go away

depend   to trust someone or something to give you the help you need
The blind man depends on his guide dog.

depress   to make someone feel sad

depth   how deep something is

descend   (*say* di-send) to go down

describe   to say what something or someone is like

description   words that tell you about someone or something

desert   (*say* dez-ert) dry land where very few plants can grow

deserted   left by everyone
a deserted house

deserve   to have done something that makes people think you should get a reward or a punishment
He was so brave he deserves a medal.

design   to draw a plan or pattern for something

desire   to want very much

desk   a kind of table where you can read, write, and keep books

despair   to give up hope
She despaired of learning Chinese.

desperate   ready to do even dangerous or stupid things, because you have lost hope
a desperate robber

despise   to dislike someone because they are bad and you think you are much better than they are
They despised him because he had cheated.

dessert   (*say* di-zert) sweet food eaten after the main part of a meal

destination   the place you are travelling to

destroy   **1** to damage something so badly that it cannot be used again **2** to kill a very sick animal that cannot be cured

destroyer   a small, fast ship for attacking other ships

destruction   when something is destroyed

detail a tiny piece of information about something
She could remember every detail about the house.

detective someone who tries to find out who did a murder or robbery

determined with your mind firmly made up
determined to win

detest to hate

develop to become bigger or better

device something that has been made for a special purpose
A can-opener is a useful device.

dew tiny drops of water that form during the night on things outside

diagonal a slanting line drawn from one corner of something to the opposite corner

diagram a kind of picture that explains something
The car book had a diagram of an engine.

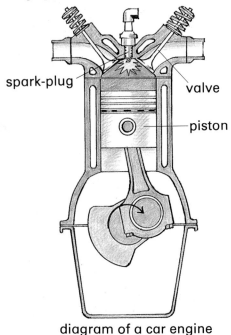

spark-plug

valve

piston

diagram of a car engine

dial a circle with numbers or letters round it. Clocks, watches, and telephones have dials.

dialect the way people living in a particular place speak

diameter the distance across a circle, through the centre

diamond **1** a very hard jewel like clear glass
2 a shape with four sloping sides that are the same length. Some playing-cards have red diamonds printed on them. (See picture on p. 222)

diary a book where you can write down what happens every day

dice a small cube used in games. Each side is marked with a different number of spots from 1 to 6.

dictionary a book where you can find out what a word means and how to spell it

did see **do**

die to stop living
The dog was dying.
The king had died.

diet special meals that some people must have to be healthy

difference how different one thing is from another thing

different not like someone or something else

difficult not easy
a difficult sum

difficulty **1** something difficult
2 *with difficulty* not easily

dig to move soil away to make a hole in the ground
I dug a hole and planted the tree.

digest to change the food in your stomach so your body can use it

dignified   looking serious and important
The mayor looked dignified.

dim   not bright

dimple   a small hollow in the cheek or chin

dinghy   (*say* ding-ee) a small boat

dingy   (*say* din-jee) looking dirty
a dingy room

dining-room   the room where people have their meals

dinner   the main meal of the day

dinosaur   a large animal that lived millions of years ago

dinosaurs

direct   **1** to show someone the way   **2** as straight and quick as it can be
the direct route

direction   the way you go to get somewhere

dirt   dust or mud

dirty   marked with dirt or stains
a dirty face

disagree   to think that someone else is wrong and you are right

disappear   to go away and not be seen any more

disappoint   to make someone sad by not doing what they hoped

disaster   something very bad that happens suddenly

disc   **1** any round, flat object   **2** a record
I'll play a disc on my record player.

discs (2)

disciple   a follower of a great teacher or a religious leader

discourage   to try to stop someone doing something by telling them how difficult or foolish it is
They discouraged him from rock-climbing.

discover   to find out about something

discovery   finding out about something

discuss   to talk about something with people who have different ideas about it

disease   illness

disgraceful   so bad that it brings you shame
disgraceful work

disguise   to make yourself look different so that people will not recognize you
The thief disguised himself as a policeman.

disgust   to be so nasty that people hate it

dishonest   not honest

disk   a device for storing a lot of data for a computer

disk drive   a device for reading a computer disk in the same way that a turntable plays a record

disk drive

dislike   to feel that you do not like someone or something

dismal   dark and sad
The weather was dismal – cold, wet, and grey.

dismay   to make someone lose hope and be afraid
He was dismayed to find he was still lost and it was nearly night.

dismiss   to send someone away
The teacher dismissed the class at the end of the day.

display   1 to show
The class displayed their work.
2 a show
a dancing display

dissolve   to mix something into a liquid so that it becomes part of the liquid. You can dissolve salt in water very easily.

distance   the amount of space between two places
The teacher asked the children to estimate the distance between the two trees.

distant   far away

distinct   1 easy to see or hear
The cuckoo call was quite distinct.
2 different
Each type of pig has distinct colours.

distress   great sorrow, trouble, or worry

district   part of a town, city, county, or country

disturb   1 to upset someone's peace or rest
2 to move something out of place

disturbance   something that upsets someone's peace or rest

ditch   a long, narrow channel. Ditches are dug to take away water from land.

divan   a low bed

dive   to jump head first into water

divide   1 to share something out
2 to split something into smaller parts
3 to find out how many times one number goes into another. Six divided by two is three,
$6 \div 2 = 3$.

divorce   the ending of a marriage

dizzy   feeling as if everything is spinning round you

do **1** to carry out an action
She does her sewing neatly.
Don't cry. What are you doing?
2 to finish
I did my work before I went out to play. He didn't.
Have you done your picture yet?

dock a place where ships and boats are loaded, unloaded, or mended

doctor someone whose job is to help sick people to get better

dodge to move quickly to get out of the way of something

doe a female deer, rabbit, or hare

does see **do**

doll a toy in the shape of a person

dollar an amount of money. Dollars are used in the United States of America, Australia, and some other countries.

dolphin an animal with warm blood that lives in the sea

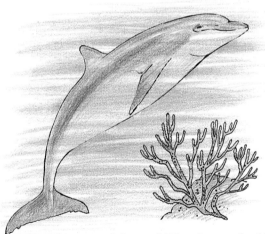

dome a roof shaped like the top half of a ball. St. Paul's Cathedral has a dome.

domino a small, oblong piece of wood or plastic with spots on it. You use twenty-eight dominoes to play the game called **dominoes**

done see **do**

donkey an animal that looks like a small horse with long ears

donkeys

doodle to scribble while you are thinking about something else

dose the amount of medicine someone has to take

double twice as much or as many

doubt (*rhymes with* out)
the feeling you have when you are not sure about something

doubtful not sure

dough (*rhymes with* so)
a mixture of flour and water. Dough is used for making bread and cakes.

doughnut a small cake that is fried and covered in sugar

dove a bird that looks like a small pigeon

down **1** to somewhere lower
Run down the hill.
2 very soft feathers

downward, downwards moving to somewhere lower

doze to be nearly asleep

dozen   a set of twelve

drab   looking dull
drab clothes

drag   to pull something heavy along

dragon   a monster with wings, that you read about in stories. Dragons breathe out fire and often guard treasure.

dragonfly   a brightly coloured insect that lives near water

drain   **1** a pipe for taking away water
2 to get rid of water by using pipes or ditches

drake   a male duck

drama   acting in a play or story

drank   see **drink**

draught   (*rhymes with* raft)
1 cold air that blows into a room
2 one of twenty-four round pieces used in the game of **draughts**

draw   **1** to do a picture with a pen, pencil, or crayon
2 to end a game with the same score as the other side
They drew 1–1 last Saturday.

drawbridge   a bridge over the water round a castle. It can be pulled up to stop people getting into the castle.

drawer   a box without a lid, that slides into a piece of furniture

drawn   see **draw**

dread   great fear
Cats have a dread of water.

dreadful   very bad
dreadful weather

dream   to see and hear things while you are asleep
Last night I dreamt about Christmas.

drench   to make someone very wet all over
He was drenched by the rain.

dress   **1** to put clothes on
2 a piece of clothing that is like a skirt and blouse in one

drew   see **draw**

dribble   **1** to let liquid come out of your mouth without meaning to. Babies often dribble.
2 to keep kicking a ball as you run along, so that the ball stays close to your feet
He dribbled the ball a little way and then passed.

drift   to be carried gently along by water or air

drill   a tool for making holes

drink   to swallow liquid
Have you drunk your milk?
He was thirsty, so he drank a lot.

drip   to let drops of liquid fall

drive to make a machine or animal move
He's never driven a bus before.
I drove the cows into the field.
He was driving too fast.

drizzle very light rain

droop to hang down weakly
a drooping flower

drop 1 a tiny amount of liquid
a drop of blood
2 to let something fall

drove see **drive**

drown to die because you are under water and cannot breathe

drowsy sleepy

drum a hollow musical instrument that you bang

drums

drunk see **drink**

dry not damp or wet
dry land

duchess a woman married to a duke

duck 1 a bird that lives near water. It has a wide, flat beak.
2 to bend down quickly to get out of the way

due 1 expected
The train is due now.
2 *due to* caused by
The accident was due to the fog.

duel a fight between two people using the same kind of weapon
a duel with swords

duffel-coat a thick coat with a hood and long, narrow buttons that go through loops

dug see **dig**

duke a very important nobleman

dull 1 not interesting
a dull book
2 not bright
a dull colour
3 not sharp
a dull sound

dumb not able to speak

dummy 1 a piece of rubber made for a baby to suck
2 a model of a person. You often see dummies in shop windows.

dump 1 a place where rubbish is left
2 to leave something you want to get rid of
3 to put something down carelessly
She dumped her school-bag on the table.

dungeon (*say* dunjun)
a prison underneath a building

during while something else is going on
I fell asleep during the film.

dusk the dim light at the end of the day, just before it gets dark

dust 1 dry dirt that is like powder
2 to clear dust away from something

dustbin a large container with a lid, for rubbish

duty what you ought to do
A soldier's duty is to fight for his country.

duvet (*say* doovay)
a cover for a bed instead of blankets

dwarf a very small person or thing

dwindle to get smaller and smaller
The crowd dwindled away once the rain started.

dye to change the colour of something by putting it in a special liquid
He dyed his hair orange.

dying see **die**

dynamite something very powerful that is used for blowing things up
a stick of dynamite

E e

each every
Each child had a cake.

eager full of a strong wish to do something
They were eager to start the race.

eagle a large bird that eats other animals

ear 1 the part of the head used for hearing
2 the group of seeds at the top of a stalk of corn

early 1 near the beginning
early in the day
2 sooner than we expected
She came early.

earn to get money by working for it

earth 1 the planet that we all live on
2 soil

earthquake a time when the ground suddenly shakes. Strong earthquakes can destroy buildings.

ease rest from pain and trouble

easel a stand for holding a blackboard or a picture

east in the direction of the rising sun

Easter the time when Christians remember that Jesus Christ came back from the dead

eastern from the east or in the east

easy 1 able to be done or understood without any trouble
2 comfortable

eat to take food into the body
Has he eaten his dinner?
He ate it all five minutes ago.

eccentric likely to behave in a strange way

echo a sound that is heard again as it bounces back off something solid. Echoes are often heard in caves and tunnels.

eclipse 1 a time when the moon comes between the earth and the sun so that the sun's light cannot be seen
2 a time when the earth comes between the sun and the moon so that the moon's light cannot be seen

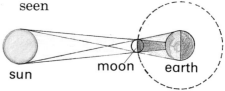

eclipse 1

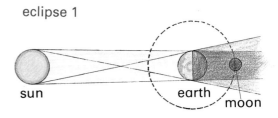

eclipse 2

edge   the part along the end or side of something

edit   **1** to get a newspaper, magazine, or book ready for printing
2 to put a story, film, or tape-recording in the order you want

editor   the person in charge of a newspaper, magazine, or comic. Editors decide which stories and pictures will be printed.

education   the teaching and training people get in schools and colleges

eel   a fish that looks like a snake (See picture on p. 220)

effect   anything that happens because of something else
The effect of the snow was that the roads were blocked.

effort   hard work at something you are trying to do

egg   **1** an oval object with a thin shell, made by a hen and used as food
2 one of the oval objects that baby birds, fish, insects, or snakes live inside until they are big enough to be born

eiderdown   a large, cloth bag filled with something soft like feathers and used as a cover for a bed

either   one or the other of two people or things
It's either right or wrong.

elastic   a strip of material that can stretch in length and then go back to its usual size

elbow   the bony part in the middle of the arm where it bends

elder   older than another person
She is the elder of the two sisters.

election   a time when people can choose the men and women who will be in charge of their town or country
a General Election

electric   worked by electricity

electricity   power that moves along wires. Electricity is used for giving light and heat and for making machines work.

electron   something very tiny that carries electricity

electronic   worked by electrons

elephant   a very big grey animal with tusks and a very long nose, called a trunk, that it uses like an arm

elephants

elf   a kind of fairy
two elves

elm   a kind of tall tree (See picture on p. 219)

else   besides
Ask someone else.

embark   to get on a ship at the beginning of a journey

embarrass   to make someone feel shy and upset

embrace   to put your arms round someone

embroidery   pretty sewing that decorates something

emerald   a green jewel

emergency   something very dangerous that suddenly happens

emigrate   to go and live in another country

emperor   a man who rules over a group of countries

empire   a group of countries ruled over by one person

employ   to pay someone to work for you

empress   **1** a woman who rules over a group of countries
2 the wife of an emperor

empty   with nothing in it or on it

enamel   **1** a kind of paint that gives a hard, shiny surface to things
2 the hard, shiny surface of your teeth

encourage   to make someone brave and full of hope so that they will do something
He encouraged her to dive from the diving-board.

encyclopedia   a book or set of books that tells you about all kinds of things

end   **1** the last part of something
2 to finish

endeavour   to try hard

enemy   **1** someone who wants to hurt you
2 the people fighting on the other side

energetic   full of the strength for doing a lot of things

energy   the strength to do things

engine   a machine that makes its own power and is used to make things move

engineer   someone who plans the building of roads, bridges, or machines

enjoy   to like watching, listening to, or doing something

enormous   very big

enough   as much as is needed
enough money

enter   **1** to come or go in
2 to take part in a race or a competition

entertain   to make time pass very pleasantly for people
The clown entertained the children.

entertainment   anything that entertains people. Shows, circuses, plays, and films are entertainments.

enthusiasm   a very great interest in something
an enthusiasm for football

enthusiastic   so interested in something that you spend a lot of time on it and are always talking about it

entire   whole
The entire class was ill.

entrance   the way into a place

entry   **1** a way into a place
the entry to the tunnel
2 going or coming into a place
a 'No Entry' sign
3 a person, animal, or thing in a competition
There were many entries for the cat show competition.

envelope   a paper cover for a letter

envious   full of envy

environment   everything around you that affects how you live and develop
Pollution is a danger to the environment.

envy   a feeling you get when you would like to have something that someone else has

equal   the same as something else in amount, size, or value
They had equal shares of the cake.

equator   an imaginary line round the middle of the earth. Countries near the equator are very hot.

equipment   the things you need for doing something

erect   upright

errand   a short journey to take a message or fetch something for someone

error   a mistake

escalator   a moving staircase

escape   **1** to get free
The prisoner escaped.
2 to get away
They escaped from the rain by going into a café.

Eskimo   *(also called* Innuit*)*
one of the people who live in very cold parts of North America, Greenland, and Russia

Eskimo people

especially   more than anything else

estate   **1** an area of land with a lot of houses on it
a housing estate
2 a large area of land that belongs to one person

estimate   to guess the amount, size, or price

ethnic   about one particular race or group of people

eve   the day or night before a special day
Christmas Eve

even   **1** level or equal
Our scores were even.
2 a number two will go into
Six is an even number.

evening   the time at the end of the day before people go to bed

event   something important that happens
Your birthday is an important event.

eventually   in the end

ever   **1** at any time
Have you ever read this?
2 *for ever* always

evergreen   any tree that has green leaves all through the year

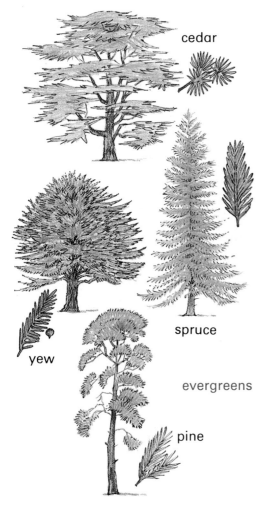

cedar

yew

spruce

evergreens

pine

every   each
Every week has seven days.

everybody, everyone   every person

everything   all things

everywhere   in all places

evil   very wicked
an evil deed

ewe   (*say* you)
a female sheep

exact   just right

exaggerate   to make something sound bigger than it is
He exaggerated the size of the fish he caught.

exam, examination   an important test

examine   to look at something very carefully

example   **1** anything that shows how something works or what it is like
The class copied the example from the book.
2 a person or thing that should be copied
He behaves so well he sets a good example.

excellent   very good

except   apart from
Everyone got a prize except me.

exchange   to give something and get something in return

excite   to interest someone so much that they have strong feelings such as love, fear, or anger
an exciting film

excitement   an excited feeling

exclaim   to make a sudden sound because you are surprised or excited

exclamation mark   a mark like this ! put after words to show that they have been shouted or are surprising

excursion   a trip out somewhere for the day or afternoon
an excursion to the seaside

excuse[1]   (*ends in the sound* —s)
words that try to explain why you have done wrong so that you will not get into trouble
Her excuse for being late was that she had missed the bus.

excuse[2] *(ends in the sound —z)* to forgive

execute to kill someone as a punishment
In some countries murderers are executed.

exercise **1** work that makes your body healthy and strong
Take exercise to keep fit.
2 a piece of work that you do to make yourself better at something
Do this exercise to practise your handwriting.

exhausted tired out

exhibition a group of things put on show so that people can come to see them
an exhibition of paintings

exile someone who has to live away from their own country

exist **1** to be real, not imaginary
Do fairies exist?
2 to live

exit the way out of a place

expand to get bigger. A balloon expands when you blow air into it.

expect to think something is very likely to happen
It is so cold I expect it will snow.

expedition a journey made in order to do something
a climbing expedition

expensive with a high price
an expensive car

experience **1** what you have learnt from things that you have seen and done
The experience of living on a farm has made him fond of all animals.
2 something that has happened to you
a frightening experience

experiment a test to find out whether an idea works

an experiment

expert someone who does something very well or knows a lot about something

explain to make something clear to people so that they understand it

explanation something said or written to help people to understand

explode to make something burst or blow up with a loud bang
Bombs explode.

explore to look carefully round a place for the first time

explosion a loud bang made by something bursting or blowing up

explosive anything used for making things blow up

express **1** a fast train
2 to put an idea or feeling into words
He expressed his regret that he could not help.

expression the look on someone's face

extension a part that has been added to make something bigger
a kitchen extension

extent the length or area of something
The train set covered the full extent of the bedroom floor.

extinguish to put out a fire

extra more than usual

extraordinary very unusual

extravagant always ready tospend much more money than people think you ought

extreme 1 very great
extreme cold
2 the furthest away
the extreme north

eye 1 the part of the head used for seeing
2 the small hole in a needle

eye 1

eyebrow the curved line of hair above each eye

eyelash one of the short hairs that grow in a fringe around each eye

F f

fable a story about animals that teaches people something

face 1 the front part of the head
2 a surface
A cube has six faces.
3 to have the front towards something
The church is facing the school.

fact anything that people know is true

factory a building where machines are used to make things

fade 1 to lose colour
faded curtains
2 to get paler or quieter so that it is harder to see or hear
The music faded at the end of the tape.

Fahrenheit (*say* farren-hite)
a way of measuring temperature that gives 32 degrees for freezing water and 212 degrees for boiling water

fail to try to do something but not be able to do it

failure someone or something that has failed

faint 1 weak
a faint cry
2 to feel so dizzy that everything goes black and you fall down

fair 1 light in colour
fair hair
2 right or just
It's not fair.
3 a group of roundabouts, stalls, shows, and games that come together in a place for a few days

fair 3

fairly **1** without cheating
Play fairly.
2 almost or quite
fairly good, I'm fairly sure.

fairy one of the tiny, magic people in stories

faith belief in someone or something

faithful always ready to help your friends and do what you have promised to do

fake something not valuable that is made to look valuable
The painting was a fake.

fall to come down suddenly
He's fallen off his bike.
I fell over yesterday.

false **1** not real
false teeth
2 not true
a false friend

falter **1** to keep stopping and nearly falling over
The baby faltered when she tried walking on her own.
2 to keep stopping while you are speaking
Her voice faltered as she spoke to the large crowd.

fame being famous
great fame

familiar well known to you
a familiar face

family parents and their children and grandchildren

famine a time when there is very little food

famous very well known

fancy **1** decorated
a fancy hat
2 *fancy dress* unusual dressing-up clothes
3 to want
I fancied an ice-cream.

fang a long, sharp tooth. Dogs, wolves, and poisonous snakes have fangs.

far a long way
far from home

fare the money people have to pay to travel on trains, buses, boats, or aeroplanes

farewell goodbye

farm a piece of land where someone grows crops and keeps animals for food

farmer someone who keeps a farm

farther to a greater distance
I live farther away now.

fashion the up-to-date way of dressing most people like and try to copy

fast **1** moving quickly
a fast car
2 quickly
Don't drive too fast.
3 firmly fixed
It was stuck fast in the mud.
4 showing a time that is later than the correct time. Watches and clocks are sometimes fast.
5 to have nothing to eat for a time

fasten **1** to close something so that it will not come open
Fasten the seat-belt.
2 to join to something
Fasten a label on the bag.

fastener   something used for fastening things
a zip-fastener

fat   **1** with a very thick, round body
2 the white, greasy part of meat
3 any grease that is used in cooking. Butter, margarine, and lard are fats.

fatal   causing death
a fatal accident

father   a male parent

fault   something wrong that spoils a person or thing

favour   something kind that you do for someone

favourite   liked the most

fawn   **1** a young deer
2 a light brown colour

fawn 1

fear   **1** a feeling you get when you think something bad might happen to you
2 to be afraid of someone or something

feast   a special meal for a lot of people

feat   something brave or difficult that has been done
Climbing the mountain was a daring feat.

feather   one of the many light, flat parts that cover a bird instead of hair or fur

fed   see **feed**

feeble   weak

feed   **1** to give food to a person or animal
I fed the cat last night.
2 to eat
The pigs are feeding now.

feel   **1** to touch something to find out what it is like
2 to know something inside yourself

feeling   something that you feel inside yourself, like anger or love

feet   more than one **foot**

fell   see **fall**

felt   **1** see **feel**
2 a kind of cloth made from wool

female   any person or animal that can become a mother

feminist   someone who believes that women should have the same opportunities in life as men

fence   a kind of wall made of wood or posts and wire. Fences are put round gardens and fields.

fern   a plant with leaves like feathers and no flowers

ferret   a small animal used for catching rats and rabbits

ferry   a boat that takes people from one side of a piece of water to the other

fertile   able to make a lot of healthy plants
fertile soil

festival   a time when people do special things to show that they are happy about something

fetch   to go and get

fête   (*rhymes with* date)
a kind of party in the open air with competitions and stalls selling different things
At the fête there was a lucky dip.

fever   an illness that makes people feel very hot and dizzy

few   not many

fiddle   **1** a violin
2 to play about with something
She fiddled with her pencil during the story.

fidget   to keep moving because you cannot keep still
The excited class fidgeted on the floor waiting for the news.

field   a piece of ground with a fence around it and crops or grass growing on it

fierce   angry and cruel

fight   to take part in a struggle, battle, or war

figure   **1** one of the signs for numbers, such as 1, 2, and 3
2 the shape of a body

file   **1** a line of people one behind the other
Line up in single file.
2 a flat tool that is rubbed against things to make them smooth
A nail-file will keep your nails smooth.

fill   to make someone or something full

film   **1** a piece or roll of thin plastic put in a camera for taking photographs
2 moving photographs with sound that tell a story

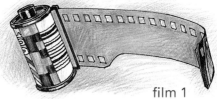

film 1

filthy   very dirty

fin   one of the thin, flat parts that stand out from a fish's body and helps it swim (See picture on p. 220)

find   to come across something, either by chance or because you have been looking for it
I've found my coat.

fine   **1** very thin
fine material
2 dry and sunny
fine weather
3 very good
a fine picture
4 money someone has to pay as a punishment
a parking fine

finger   one of the five separate parts at the end of the hand

fingerprint   the mark left on the surface of something by the tip of a finger

finish   to come to the end of something

fir   a tall tree that has cones and leaves that look like green needles

fire   **1** the heat and bright light that come from burning things
2 *to fire a gun*   to shoot

fireman   a man whose job is to put out fires

fire-place   the part of a room where the fire and hearth are

firework   a paper tube filled with a powder that will burn noisily and bang or send out coloured sparks and smoke

firm   fixed so that it will not give way

first   before all the others

fish   **1** any animal with scales and fins that always lives and breathes under water (See pictures on p. 220)
2 to try to catch fish

fisherman   someone who catches fish

fishmonger   someone who keeps a shop that sells fish

fist   a hand with all the fingers pressed in towards the palm

fit   **1** healthy
2 good enough
fit for a king
3 to be the right size and shape

fix   **1** to join firmly to something
Fix the shelf onto the wall.
2 to mend
She fixed the broken toy.

fizzy   with a lot of tiny bubbles that keep bursting
fizzy drinks

flag   a piece of coloured cloth with a pattern on it, joined to a pole. Every country has its own flag.

flags

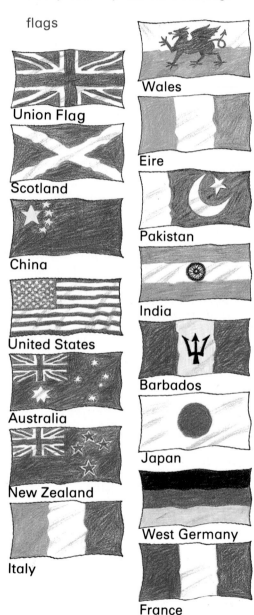

Union Flag

Scotland

China

United States

Australia

New Zealand

Italy

Wales

Eire

Pakistan

India

Barbados

Japan

West Germany

France

flake   a very thin, light piece of something
snowflakes

flame   fire that is shaped like a pointed tongue

flannel   a piece of soft cloth used for washing yourself

flap   **1** to move up and down like a bird's wings
2 a part that hangs down and is joined to the rest by one side. Envelopes have flaps.

flare   to burn with a sudden, bright flame

flash   to shine suddenly and brightly

flask   a container that keeps hot drinks hot and cold drinks cold

flat   **1** not curved and with no bumps in it
A snooker table must be perfectly flat.
2 a home that is a set of rooms inside a house or a big building
a block of flats

flatten   to make flat
The field of corn was flattened by the strong wind.

flatter   to praise someone too much
She flattered the man, saying his cooking was the best she had ever tasted.

flavour   the smell and taste of something
Which flavour of ice-cream do you like?

flea   a small jumping insect without wings that sucks blood

flee   to run away
He saw the policeman and fled.

fleece   the wool that covers a sheep

flesh   the soft stuff between the bones and skin

flew   see **fly**

flight   **1** a journey through the air
2 an escape
They made their flight from the prison as soon as it was dark.
3 *a flight of stairs* a set of stairs

flinch   to move back slightly because you are afraid

fling   to throw something as hard as you can
I flung a stone and it hit the giant.

float   **1** to be on the top of a liquid
Wood floats on water.
2 to be carried along by liquid or air
The balloon floated in the air.

flock   a group of birds or sheep that feed together

flood   a lot of water that spreads over land that is usually dry

floor   the part of a building or room that people walk on

flop   to fall or sit down suddenly
After the race she flopped down to the ground.

floppy disk   a device for storing a large amount of information for a computer

flour   a powder made from wheat and used for making bread, pastry, and cakes

flourish   **1** to grow well
The plants flourished.
2 to be happy and successful
The Brownie pack is flourishing. It is getting very popular.

flow   to move along like a river
The traffic was flowing smoothly on the motorway.

flower   the part of a plant that produces seeds

flown   see **fly**

flu   an illness that gives you a cold and makes you ache all over and feel very hot

fluff   light, soft stuff that comes off wool, hair, or feathers

fluke   a piece of luck that makes you able to do something you thought you could not do
He scored the goal by a lucky fluke.

flung   see **fling**

flutter   **1** to keep moving the wings quickly, but not fly very far
2 to move a little, like a flag in a very light wind

fly   **1** to move through the air with wings or in an aeroplane
I flew from London to Paris last week.
He's never flown before.
2 a small insect with one pair of wings

foal   a young horse

foam   **1** a lot of small bubbles on the top of a liquid
2 thick, soft rubber used for making sponges

fog   damp air that looks like thick smoke and is difficult to see through

fold   to lay one part of something on top of another part

folder   a large cover made of card for keeping your work in

foliage   leaves

folk   people

follow   to go after

fond   liking someone or something a lot
fond of fish fingers

food   anything that you eat to help you grow and be healthy

fool   someone who is very silly

foolish   silly

foot   **1** the part joined to the lower end of the leg
two feet
2 a measure for length

football   a game played by two teams who kick a ball and try to score goals

footprint   the mark left by a foot

footsteps   the sound your feet make as you walk or run

forbid   to say that someone must not do something
She was forbidden to go out.

force   **1** to use your power to make a person, animal, or thing do something
The man forced open the door.
2 a group of people with weapons
3 power
The force of his punch knocked out the other boxer.

forecast   saying what you think is going to happen before it happens
a weather forecast

forehead   the part of the face above the eyebrows

foreign belonging to another country
foreign coins

forest a lot of trees growing together

forgave see **forgive**

forge 1 to write or paint like someone else to deceive people
She forged his signature.
2 to make a copy of something and pretend it is real
3 a place where metal is heated and shaped
In the blacksmith's forge horseshoes are made.

forge 3

forgery writing or a picture that is made to look as if someone else has done it

forget to fail to remember
I've forgotten my dinner money.
I forgot the time and was late.

forgive to stop being angry with someone
Have you forgiven me?
I forgave him when he explained.

forgot, forgotten see **forget**

fork a tool with three or four thin, pointed parts. People use small forks for picking up food and putting it into their mouths.

form 1 the shape something has
2 a long wooden seat without a back
3 one of the classes in a school
I am in Form 2.
4 a printed paper with spaces where you have to write
Fill in the form.

fort a strong building with soldiers in it, made to protect a place against its enemies

fortnight two weeks

fortress a big fort

fortunate lucky

fortune 1 a lot of money
He won a fortune at bingo.
2 luck
She set out to seek her fortune.

forward, forwards in the direction you are facing

fossil any part of a dead plant or animal that has been in the ground millions of years and become hard like rock

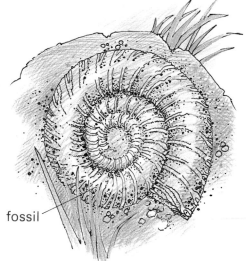

fossil

foster-mother a woman who takes a child to live with her family while the child's parents cannot look after them

71

fought   see **fight**

foul   dirty and bad

found   see **find**

foundations   the solid part under the ground that a building is built on

fountain   water that shoots up into the air

fowl   any bird that is kept for its meat or eggs, like a hen

fox   a wild animal that looks like a dog and has a long, furry tail

fraction   **1** a number that is not a whole number. ½, ⅗, and ¼ are fractions.
2 a very small part of something

fragile   easily broken
Glass is fragile.

fragment   a small piece that has been broken off
fragments of rock

frame   something that fits round the edge of a picture

fraud   a trick or a person who tries to cheat someone

freak   any person, animal, or thing with something very strange about it

freckle   one of the small brown spots people sometimes get on their skin when they have been in the sun

free   **1** with nothing to stop you doing something or going somewhere
2 not costing anything
a free gift

freeze   **1** to change into ice
The pond froze last night.
2 to be very cold
Your hands will be frozen.

freezer   a large refrigerator used for keeping food very cold for a long time

frequent   happening often
frequent rain

fresh   **1** not old, tired, or used
fresh air, fresh bread,
a fresh start
2 not tinned
fresh fruit

fret   to keep worrying and getting upset about something
The dog fretted when its owners went away.

fridge   short for **refrigerator**

friend   someone you like who likes you. Friends like doing things together.

frieze   a wide strip of pictures along the top of a wall
an alphabet frieze in the classroom

fright   sudden fear

frighten   to make someone afraid

frill   a strip of material with tiny pleats in it. Frills are stitched to the edges of things to decorate them.

fringe   short hair brushed forward on to the forehead

fritter   a slice of potato, fruit, or meat dipped in a mixture of egg, flour, and milk and then fried

frog   a small animal with a smooth, wet skin. Frogs live near water and can swim and jump.

from   out of

front   the side that people usually see or come to first
front door

frost   ice that looks like powder and covers things when the weather is very cold

froth   a lot of small bubbles on the top of a liquid

frown   to have lines on your forehead because you are angry or worried

froze, frozen   see **freeze**

fruit   the seed of a plant and the soft or juicy part round it (See pictures on p. 217)

fry   to cook in hot fat in a pan on top of a stove
He fried the eggs.

frying-pan   a large, shallow pan

fudge   a kind of soft, very sweet toffee

fuel   anything that is burnt to make heat
Coal is a fuel.

full   with no more room

fund   money that will be used for something special
We must raise funds for the school trip.

funeral   the time when a dead person's body is buried or burnt

fungus   a kind of plant that is not green and grows in damp places. Mushrooms and toadstools are both **fungi**.

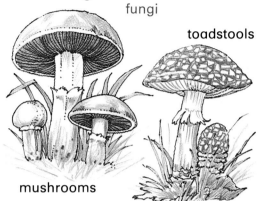

fungi

toadstools

mushrooms

funnel   **1** a chimney on a ship or railway engine (See picture on p. 215)
2 a tube with one very wide end to help you pour things into bottles
Pour the oil through a funnel.

funny   **1** amusing
a very funny joke
2 strange
a funny smell

fur   the soft hair that covers some animals

furious   very angry

furniture   things such as beds and tables that you need inside a house and can move about

furrow   the straight, narrow hollow made in the ground by a plough

furry   covered in fur

further   to a greater distance
I swam further than you.

fuse   **1** a piece of cord used for setting off an explosion
2 a small piece of wire that will melt to stop too much electricity going through. Most plugs have fuses in them.

fuss   to worry and bother too much about something that is not important.

future   the time that will come

G g

gabble   to talk so quickly that it is difficult for other people to understand what you are saying

gadget   a small, useful tool
A penknife is a useful gadget.

gain   to get something that you did not have before

galaxy   a very large group of stars that belong together, such as the Milky Way

gale   a very strong wind

galleon   a Spanish ship with sails, used long ago

gallery   1 a building or long room where paintings are shown
an art gallery
2 the upstairs seats in a theatre or church

galley   1 a large boat used long ago that needed a lot of men to row it
2 the kitchen on a ship

gallon   a measure for liquid
eight pints = one gallon

gallop   to move like a horse moving very quickly

gamble   to try to win money by playing a game that needs luck

game   something that you play at that has rules. Football and draughts are games.

gander   a male goose

gang   a group of people who do things together

gangster   someone who belongs to a gang that robs and kills people

gangway   1 the plank or set of steps that people walk up to get on to a boat
2 the path between rows of seats in a large building, such as in a cinema

gaol   (*say* jail)
prison

gape   1 to have your mouth wide open with surprise
He gaped when he saw his best friend on television.
2 to be wide open
The workmen left a gaping hole in the road.

garage   1 the building where a car or bus is kept
2 a place that sells petrol and mends cars

garden   a piece of ground where flowers, fruit, or vegetables are grown

gargle   to wash your throat by moving liquid around inside it then spitting it out

garter   a band of elastic put round a sock to keep it up

gas **1** anything that is like air. Some gases have strong smells.
2 a gas that is burnt to make heat

gash a deep cut

gasp to breathe in noisily and quickly because you are surprised or ill
gasping for breath

gate a kind of door in a wall or fence round a piece of land

gather **1** to bring together
The children gathered in front of the teacher.
2 to pick
Let's gather blackberries.

gave see **give**

gay **1** cheerful
a gay tune
2 brightly coloured
gay curtains

gaze to look at something for a long time

gear **1** the things needed for a job or sport
camping gear
2 part of a bicycle or car. Gears help to control the speed of the wheels so that it is easier to go up and down hills.

geese more than one **goose**

gem a valuable or beautiful stone

general **1** belonging to most people or things
The general weather forecast gives an idea of the weather for the whole country.
2 an important officer in the army
A general is in charge of many soldiers.

generous always ready to give or share what you have

gentle quiet and kind

gentleman a polite name for a man
Ladies and gentlemen . . .

genuine real
Is that diamond genuine?

geography finding out about different parts of the world

geranium a plant with red, pink, or white flowers that is often grown in a pot (See picture on p. 218)

gerbil (*begins with the sound* j—) a small, pale brown animal with long back legs and very soft fur. Gerbils dig holes in sand and are often kept as pets.

germ something that is alive but too small to see and that makes people ill

get **1** to become
My cat is getting old.
2 to take, buy, or be given something
I got a new bike yesterday.
I'm getting one for my birthday.

ghost the shape of a dead person that people think they have seen moving as if he were alive

giant one of the very big people in fairy stories

giddy   dizzy

gift   a present
   a birthday gift

gigantic   (*say* jy-gantic)   very big

giggle   to keep laughing in a silly way because you cannot stop yourself

gill   the part on each side of a fish that it breathes through
   (See picture on p. 220)

ginger   a powder that gives a strong, hot taste to things

gingerbread   sticky cake or thick biscuit that tastes of ginger

gipsy   one of a group of people with dark hair and skin, who do not live in houses but travel from place to place in caravans. Gipsies are also called travellers.

giraffe   a very tall African animal with a very long neck

girl   a female child or teenager

give   to let someone have something
   Dad gave me this yesterday.
   She was given first prize.
   I'm giving you a second chance.

glacier   a river of ice that moves very slowly down a mountain

glad   happy

glance   to look at something quickly

glare   **1** to look angrily at someone
   2 a very strong light
   The glare of the sun hurt my eyes.

glass   **1** something hard that you can see through. Glass is used for making windows.
   2 a kind of cup that is made of glass and has no handle

glasses   a pair of glass lenses held in front of the eyes by a frame that fits over the nose and ears. People wear glasses to help them to see better.

glen   a narrow valley in Scotland and Ireland

glide   to move very smoothly
   gliding on skates

glider   a kind of aeroplane without an engine

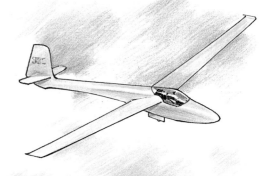

glimmer   a very weak light
   There was a glimmer of light at the end of the tunnel.

glimpse   to see something for only a few seconds
She glimpsed the school from the window of the train.

glint   to shine with a bright light that comes and goes.
Gold glints.

glisten   to shine like something with drops of water on it

glitter   to shine with a bright light that keeps coming and going
glittering jewels

globe   a ball with the map of the whole world on it

gloomy   **1** dark
a gloomy room
2 sad
a gloomy face

glory   **1** great fame
2 great beauty

glossy   smooth and shiny

glove   a covering for the hand with separate parts for the thumb and each finger

glow   to shine with the warm light a fire has

glue   a thick liquid for sticking things together

glum   not pleased or happy
He looked glum.

glutton   someone who eats too much

gnarled   (*say* narled)
twisted like the trunk of an old tree

gnat   (*say* nat)
a small fly that sucks blood

gnaw   (*say* naw)
to keep biting something hard like a bone

gnome   (*say* nome)
a kind of ugly fairy

go   to move in any direction
His car goes very fast.
She's gone out to play.
They went on holiday yesterday.
When are you going?

goal   **1** the two posts the ball must go between to score a point in games like football
2 a point scored in football, netball, and other games

goat   an animal kept for its meat and milk. Goats often have a strong smell.

gobble   to eat very quickly and greedily

goblin   a kind of bad, ugly fairy

goes   see **go**

go-kart   a kind of small, simple racing car

go-karts

gold   a valuable, shiny, yellow metal

golden   coloured like gold

goldfish   a small orange fish often kept as a pet

golf   a game played by hitting small, white balls with sticks, called clubs, over a large area of ground

gone   see **go**

good   **1** what people like and praise
good work
2 kind and true
a good friend
3 well behaved
a good boy

goodbye the word you say when you are leaving someone

goods things that can be bought and sold

goose a large bird that is kept for its meat and eggs
two geese

geese

gooseberry a green berry that grows on a bush with thorns and can be cooked and eaten

gorgeous 1 very attractive
2 with bright colours

gorilla an African animal like a very large monkey with long arms and no tail

gorse a prickly bush with small yellow flowers

gosling a young goose

gossip 1 to talk a lot in a friendly way to someone
2 to talk a lot about other people

got see **get**

govern to be in charge of a place

government the group of people who are in charge of what happens in a country

grab to take hold of something suddenly

grace 1 beautiful movements
The girl danced with grace.
2 a short prayer before or after a meal

gradual happening a little at a time

grain seed that grows in plants like corn and is used for making food

gram a tiny measure for weight
1000 gram = 1 kilogram

grand large, important, or wonderful

grandchild the child of a son or daughter. **Granddaughters** and **grandsons** are grandchildren.

grandfather the father of a father or mother

grandmother the mother of a father or mother

granite a very hard rock

grant to agree to give someone what they have asked for

grape a small, soft green or purple fruit that grows in bunches

grapefruit a fruit that looks like a big orange, but is yellow

graph a diagram that helps you to see how numbers or amounts of things are different from each other

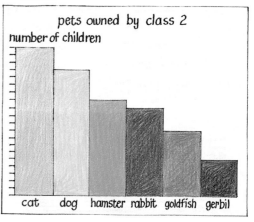

pets owned by class 2
number of children

cat dog hamster rabbit goldfish gerbil

grasp   to get hold of something and hold it tightly

grass   a green plant with flat, narrow leaves that can be eaten by cattle and other animals

grasshopper   an insect that makes a shrill sound by rubbing one leg against a wing and can jump a long way

grate   **1** a container made of metal bars. Grates hold the coal or wood in a fire.
2 to rub something against a rough surface so that it falls into tiny pieces
Grate the cheese.
3 to make the kind of noise the nail on your finger makes if you rub it against a blackboard
a grating noise

grateful   wanting to thank someone for what they have done
He was grateful for her help.

grave   **1** the hole in which a dead person is buried
2 very serious

gravel   a mixture of sand and tiny stones

gravity   the force that pulls everything towards the earth. If there was no gravity everyone would fall off the earth and float out into space.

gravy   a hot brown liquid poured over meat before it is eaten

graze   **1** to hurt the skin by rubbing hard against something
2 to eat grass as it grows. Cows and sheep graze in fields.

grease   thick, slippery stuff like oil

great   **1** large
a great amount of money
2 important
a great man
3 very good
a great idea

greed   a wish for much more food or money than you really need

greengrocer   someone who keeps a shop that sells fruit and vegetables

greenhouse   a glass building for growing plants in

greet   to welcome someone or say hello

grew   see **grow**

grief   a very sad feeling

grill   to cook food on metal bars put under or over heat

grim   **1** not looking kind, friendly, or pleased
a grim face
2 not pleasant
grim weather

grin   a smile that shows the teeth

grind   to crush into tiny bits
The wheat was ground into flour.

grip   to hold tightly

grit   tiny bits of stone or sand

groan   to make a low sound because you are in pain or trouble

grocer   someone who keeps a shop that sells food, drink, and things like soap powder and matches

groom   **1** someone whose job is to look after horses
2 to make an animal look smart by cleaning and brushing it

groove   a long, narrow hollow. Records have grooves in them.

grope   to try to find something by feeling for it when you cannot see
In the dark she groped for the light switch.

gross   twelve dozen or 144

ground   **1** the earth
2 a piece of land
3 see **grind**

group   a number of people, animals, or things that belong together in some way

grow   **1** to become bigger
You've grown very quickly.
2 to plant something in the ground and look after it
We grew huge leeks last year.

growl   to make a deep, angry sound. Angry dogs growl.

grown   see **grow**

grub   a tiny creature that will become an insect

grudge   a bad feeling you have against someone, because you think they have harmed you

gruff   with a deep, rough voice

grumble   to keep on saying that you are not pleased about something
Stop grumbling!

grunt   to make the sound a pig makes

guard   to keep someone or something safe from other people

guardian   someone who is put in charge of a child whose parents cannot look after him

guess   to say what you think the answer is when you do not really know

guest   someone who is invited

guide   **1** someone or something that shows people which way to go
2 *guide dog* a dog trained to help a blind person

Guide   a girl who is a member of the Girl Guides Association

guilt   a feeling you have when you know you have done something wrong

guilty   full of guilt

guinea pig   a furry animal that has no tail and is kept as a pet

guitar   a musical instrument with strings across it that you play with your fingers

guitars

gulf   sea that fills a very large bend in the land

gulp   to swallow very quickly

gum   **1** the hard pink part of the mouth that holds the teeth
2 a sweet that you chew
chewing-gum

gunpowder   a black powder that explodes

gurgle   to make the noise water makes as it goes down the plug-hole in a bath

gush   to move like water rushing out of a tap

gust   a sudden rush of wind or air
A gust of wind blew the bike over.

gutter   a long, narrow hollow at the side of a street or along the edge of a roof. Gutters take away rain water.

H h

habit   anything that you do without thinking, because you have done it so often
Smoking cigarettes is a bad habit.

had   see **have**

haddock   a sea fish that can be eaten (See picture on p. 220)

haggard   looking ill and very tired
a haggard face

hail   small pieces of ice that fall from the sky like rain

hair   a soft covering that grows on the heads and bodies of people and animals

hairdresser   someone whose job is to cut people's hair, wash it, or arrange it in a special way

half   one of the two equal parts something can be divided into. It can also be written as ½.
Two halves make a whole.

hall   **1** the part inside a house near the front door
2 a very big room
a school hall
3 a large, important building or house
the Town Hall

hallo, hello   the word you say when you meet someone

Hallowe'en   the 31st October when some people think that magical things happen

halt   to stop
The train halted at the red light.

halter   a rope or strap put round an animal's head or neck so that it can be controlled

halve   to divide into two equal parts

halves   more than one **half**

hammer   a heavy tool used for hitting nails

hammock   a bed that is a piece of cloth hung from something by cords joined to each corner

hamper   **1** a big basket with a lid
a picnic hamper
2 to make it difficult for someone to do something
The puppy hampered the packing as it kept jumping into the suitcase.

hamster a small brown animal that has smooth fur and is kept as a pet

hand the part joined to the lower end of the arm

handcuffs a pair of metal rings used for locking someone's wrists together

handicap anything that makes it more difficult for you to do something
The heavy rain was a handicap to the runners.

handkerchief a square of material used for blowing the nose

handle 1 a part put on something so that you can get hold of it
2 to touch, feel, hold, or use something with your hands
Handle the kittens carefully.

handsome attractive. Men and boys can be handsome.

hang to fix the top part of something to a hook or nail
I hung up my coat and went in.

hangar a big shed for keeping an aeroplane in

hanger something used for hanging up things

happen 1 to take place
This must not happen again.
2 to do something by chance
I just happened to see it.

happiness the feeling you have when you are very pleased or enjoying yourself

happy full of happiness

harbour a place where boats can stay safely in the water when they are not out at sea

hard 1 not soft
hard ground
2 difficult
hard sums
3 severe
a hard punishment

hardly only just
hardly able to walk

hardware 1 tools, nails, wire and other things made of metal
2 the machinery of a computer

hare an animal like a big rabbit that can move very quickly

harm to hurt or spoil someone or something

harness the set of straps put over a horse's head and round its neck so that it can be controlled

harp a musical instrument. It has a large frame with strings stretched across it that are played with the fingers.

harsh   not kind or gentle
a harsh voice

harvest   the time when farmers gather in the fruit, corn, or vegetables they have grown

has   see **have**

haste   hurry
He forgot all his books in his haste.

hatch   to break out of an egg. Baby birds, insects, fish, and snakes hatch.

hatchet   a light tool for chopping

hate   to have a very strong feeling against someone or something you do not like

haughty   too proud of yourself

haul   to pull with all your strength

haunted   often visited by ghosts
a haunted house

have   **1** to own
She has a new car.
We haven't got a car.
2 to contain
The jar used to have sweets in it.
3 to enjoy or suffer
We're having a good time.
He's had an accident.

hawk   a bird that hunts and eats smaller animals

hay   dry grass used to feed animals

haze   damp or hot air that it is difficult to see through

hazel   **1** a small nut tree
2 the light brown colour of a hazel nut

head   **1** the part of a person or animal that contains the brain, eyes, and mouth
2 the person in charge

headache   a pain in the head that goes on hurting

headmaster   a man in charge of all the teachers and pupils in a school

headmistress   a woman in charge of all the teachers and pupils in a school

heal   **1** to make well again
The cream healed his sore leg.
2 to become well again
The cut healed quickly.

health   **1** how someone is feeling, either well or ill
2 good health

healthy   **1** not ill or injured in any way
2 good for people's health
healthy air

heap   an untidy pile

hear   to take in sounds through the ears
I heard you shout so I came.

heart   **1** the part of the body that makes the blood go round inside
2 the curved shape of a heart. Red hearts are printed on some playing-cards. (See picture on p. 222)

hearth   (*say* harth)
the part of the floor where the fire is

heat **1** the hot feeling that comes from the sun or a fire
The heat made them sleepy.
2 to make hot
Heat up the soup.

heath wild, flat land with small bushes, but no trees

heather a low bush with small purple, pink, or white flowers. Heather grows on heaths and moors. (See picture on p. 218)

heave to lift or pull something heavy

heaven **1** God's home
2 a very happy place

heavy weighing a lot. It is difficult to lift and carry heavy things.

hedge a kind of wall made by bushes growing close together

hedgehog a small animal covered in stiff hairs like sharp needles

heel the back part of the foot

height **1** how high something is
2 a high place
on the mountain heights

heir someone who will be given money, property, or a title when their owner dies

heiress a girl or woman who will be given money, property, or a title when their owner dies

helicopter a kind of small aeroplane that can rise straight up into the air. It has large blades that spin round on its roof.

helm the handle or wheel that is used to steer a ship (See picture on p. 215)

helmet a strong covering that protects the head

help to do something useful for someone else

helpless not able to look after yourself. Babies are completely helpless.

helter-skelter a tall slide at a fair. You go round and round as you slide down it.

hem   the edge of a piece of cloth, that is folded under and sewn down

herb   a plant used in cooking to give the food a better flavour

herd   a number of cattle that feed together

here   in or to this place
Come here!

hermit   someone who lives alone and keeps away from everyone else

hero   a boy or man who has done something very brave

heroine   a girl or woman who has done something very brave

herring   a sea fish that can be eaten (See pictures on p. 220)

herself   **1** she and no one else
2 *by herself* on her own

hesitate   to wait a little before you do or say something, because you are not sure about it

hibernate   to sleep for a long time during the cold weather. Bats, tortoises, and hedgehogs all hibernate.

hiccup   to make a sudden, sharp sound. People hiccup when they have eaten or drunk very quickly or laughed a lot.

hide   **1** to get into a place where you cannot be seen
I'm hiding over here.
I hid behind the tree last time.
2 to put into a secret place
The gold was hidden in a cave.

hiding-place   a place where someone or something is hidden

high   **1** going a long way up
a high mountain
2 a long way up
It flew high into the air.

highwayman   a man on a horse, who stopped people on the roads and robbed them. Dick Turpin was a famous highwayman.

hijack   to take control of an aeroplane while it is flying and make it go where you want it to go

hill   ground that is higher than the ground around it

himself   **1** he and no one else
2 *by himself* on his own

hinder   to get in someone's way so that it is difficult for them to do something
The crowds hindered him from getting a close look at the royal family.

Hindu   someone who believes in Hinduism

Hinduism   a religion found mostly in India

hinge   a metal fastener that joins a door to a wall and lets the door swing backwards and forwards

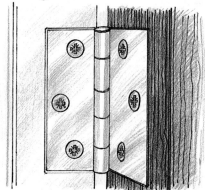

hint   **1** a useful idea
2 to give someone information without telling them exactly what you mean

hip   **1** the bony part of the body that sticks out at the side between the waist and thigh
2 a red berry on the wild rose

hippopotamus a very large, heavy, African animal that lives near water. It has tusks and very thick skin.

hippopotamuses

hire to pay to get the use of something
You can hire skates at the ice rink.

hiss to make the long sss sound that snakes make

history finding out about things that happened in the past

hive a kind of box for keeping bees in

hoard a secret store of money or other things

hoarse sounding rough and deep. People with sore throats have hoarse voices.

hobble to walk with difficulty because there is something wrong with your leg or foot

hobby something interesting that people like doing in their spare time
Gardening, stamp-collecting, and chess are all hobbies.

hoe a tool for getting rid of weeds

hold **1** to have something in your hands
I held up the picture I had done.
2 to have room inside for something
This bag will hold three books.
3 the place inside a ship where things are kept
Put the cargo in the hold.

hole a gap or opening made in something

holiday time off from school or work

hollow **1** with an empty space inside
a hollow Easter egg
2 a kind of hole
The rabbits live in a hollow under the tree.

holly a tree that has shiny, prickly leaves and red berries in the winter

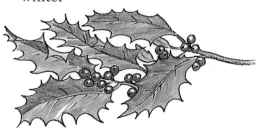

holster a case for putting a gun in. Holsters are worn on straps or belts.

holy special because it belongs to God

home the place where you live

honest not stealing, cheating, or telling lies
an honest man

honey sweet, sticky food made by bees

honour great respect

hood a covering of soft material for the head and neck

hoof the hard part round a horse's foot

hook a piece of bent metal for hanging things on or catching hold of something

hoop a big wooden or metal ring used in games

hoot to make the sound made by an owl or the horn in a car

hope to want something that you think is likely to happen

hopeless **1** very bad at doing something
He was hopeless at games.
2 without hope
It was hopeless looking for the ball in the long grass.

hopscotch a game where you hop and throw or kick a stone into squares drawn on the ground

horizon the line where the sky and the land or sea seem to meet

horizontal **1** flat and level
2 *a horizontal line* a straight line across something

horn **1** a kind of pointed bone that grows on the heads of some animals. Bulls and rams have horns.
2 a brass musical instrument that you blow into

horrible **1** nasty
a horrible sight
2 frightening
a horrible film

horrid nasty
a horrid dream

horror very great fear

horse an animal with hooves that is used for riding and pulling carts

horse-chestnut the big tree that conkers grow on (See picture on p. 219)

horseshoe a flat piece of metal fixed underneath a horse's hoof

hose-pipe a long plastic or rubber tube that water can go through

hospital a place where people who are ill or hurt are looked after

hostage someone that you hold as a prisoner or threaten with death until you get what you want

hostile being an enemy and acting in a threatening way

hotel a building where people pay to have meals and stay for the night

hound a dog used for hunting

hour sixty minutes

house a building where people live together

household all the people who live together in the same house

hover **1** to stay in one place in the air
The helicopter hovered overhead.
2 to wait near someone or something and have nothing to do
She hovered about outside the house waiting for her friend.

hovercraft a machine that is like both an aeroplane and a boat. It travels quickly just above the surface of land or water.

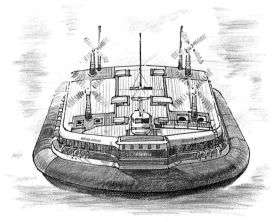

how in what way
How did you know?

howl to give a long, loud cry like an animal in pain

hub the part at the centre of a wheel, where the spokes meet

huddle to keep close to others in a group because you are cold or frightened

huge very big

hull the main part of a boat or ship
(See picture on p. 215)

hum **1** to sing a tune with your lips closed
2 to make the sound a bee makes

human any man, woman, or child

humble not proud
a humble person

humorous amusing

humour a sense of humour is when you are able to see the funny side of things

hump one of the big lumps on a camel's back

hung see **hang**

hunger the need for food

hungry feeling hunger

hunt **1** to go after a wild animal because you want to kill it
2 to look carefully for something
He hunted everywhere for the missing ring.

hurl to throw something as far as you can

hurrah, hurray a word that you shout when you are very glad about something

hurricane a storm with a very strong wind

hurry **1** to move quickly
She hurried away to catch her bus.
2 to try to do something quickly because there is not enough time
He hurried to finish as the bell had gone.

hurt to make a person or animal feel pain

hurtle to move very quickly
The rocket hurtled through space.

husband a man married to someone

hustle **1** to hurry
2 to make someone hurry
The teacher hustled the class into the hall.

hutch a kind of box for keeping a rabbit in

hyacinth a flower that grows from a bulb and has a very sweet smell

hymn a song that praises God

hyphen   a mark like this   used in writing to join parts of words together, such as pocket-money

I i

ice   **1** water that has frozen hard
2 to put icing on cakes

iceberg   a large piece of ice floating in the sea

ice-cream   a sweet, frozen food that tastes of cream

icicle   a thin, pointed piece of ice hanging down

icing   a sweet, sticky mixture spread over the tops of cakes to decorate them. Some icing goes very hard when it is dry.

idea   **1** something you have thought of yourself
2 a plan

ideal   just what you want
ideal weather for sailing

identical   exactly the same
identical twins

idiot   a very stupid person

idle   doing nothing
idle hands

idol   something people worship and treat as if it were God

igloo   a round house made of blocks of hard snow

ignition-key   the key used to start the engine of a car

ignorant   knowing nothing or only a little
an ignorant fool

ignore   to take no notice of someone

ill   not well

illness   something that makes people ill. Measles, chicken-pox, and colds are illnesses.

ill-treat   to treat badly
It is cruel to ill-treat an animal.

illuminations   a lot of bright, coloured lights used to decorate streets, buildings, or parks

illustration   a picture in a book

imaginary   not real

imagination   the ability to make pictures in your mind of things and people you cannot see

imagine   to make a picture in your mind of someone or something you cannot see

imitate   to copy a person or animal

imitation   a copy that is not as valuable as the real thing

immediately   straight away

immense   very big

impatient   not patient
The impatient man would not wait in the queue.

impertinent   rude, cheeky
an impertinent child

implore   to beg someone to do something for you
He implored his dad to buy the bike.

important   **1** powerful and worth respect
a very important person
2 worth looking at or thinking about seriously
an important notice

impossible   not possible
It is impossible to jump 10 metres.

impress   to make people think you are very good at something
She impressed her friends with her magic tricks.

impression   a vague idea or feeling
I get the impression he is lazy.

impressive   so wonderful that you will always remember it

imprison   to put someone in prison

improve   **1** to become better
Her cold is improving.
2 to make something better
He improved his handwriting.

incense   something that gives a sweet smell when it is burnt

inch   a measure for length

include   to make something part of a group of other things

incorrect   not correct

increase   **1** to make bigger
He increased the boy's pocket-money.
2 to become bigger
The bubble increased in size and then burst.

indeed   really
very wet indeed

index   a list at the back of a book. It tells you what things are in the book and where to find them.

indignant   angry because something unfair has been done or said
indignant at getting the blame

indoors   inside a building

industry   **1** hard work
2 work done in factories

infant   a young child

infectious   likely to spread to others
an infectious illness

inform   to tell someone something
She informed the police that her bag had been stolen.

information   words that tell people about something

infuriate   to make very angry
The mother was infuriated by the complaining child.

ingenious   clever at thinking of new ways of doing or making things

inhabit   to live in a place

initial   the first letter of a name
William Brown's initials are W.B.

injection   a prick in the skin made by a hollow needle filled with medicine so that the medicine goes into the body. Injections can make people better or stop them getting illnesses.

injure   to harm

injury   harm done to part of the body

ink   a coloured liquid used for writing with a pen

inland   in a part of the country that is not near the sea

inn   a kind of hotel

innings   a turn at batting in cricket

innocent   not guilty, not doing anything wrong

input   the information that is put into the memory of a computer

inquiry   **1** a question
2 a search to find out all about something

inquisitive   full of a wish to know about something. Inquisitive people often want to know about things that they have no right to know about.

insect   a tiny creature with six legs. Flies, ants, butterflies, and bees are all insects.

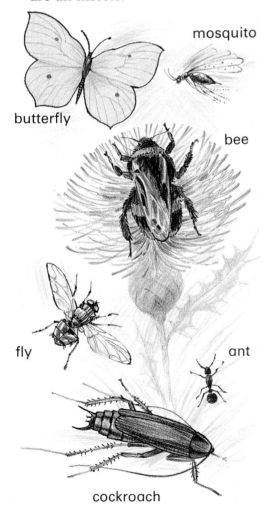

mosquito

butterfly

bee

fly

ant

cockroach

insects

inside   **1** in something
2 the part nearest the middle

insist   to be very firm in asking, saying, or doing something
He insists on staying up late.

insolent   very rude
insolent behaviour

inspect   to look carefully at people or things

inspector   **1** an important policeman
2 someone whose job is to check that things are done properly
ticket inspector

instalment   **1** a part of a story that is told in parts
a serial told in instalments
2 an amount of money people pay every week or every month in order to buy something

instantly   at once

instead   in place of something else
They made tea instead of coffee.

instinct   something that makes animals do things they have not learnt to do – they can just do it
Spiders spin webs by instinct.

instructions   words that tell people what to do

instructor   a kind of teacher
swimming instructor

instrument   **1** a tool or something else used for doing a job
2 something used for making musical sounds
A drum is a musical instrument.

insult   to hurt someone's feelings by being rude

intelligent   able to learn and understand things easily

intend   to mean to do something
Do you intend to stay?

intense   very great
intense heat

interest   to make someone want to find out more, look, or listen
A book about animals should interest most children.

interfere   **1** to get in the way
2 to take part in something that has nothing to do with you

international   belonging to more than one country
an international competition

interrupt   to stop someone from carrying on with what they are saying or doing

interval   the time between parts of a play or film
Buy an ice-cream in the interval.

interview   to ask someone questions to find out what they think about something or what they are like

introduce   to make someone known to other people
She introduced the new girl to the class.

invade   to go into another country to fight against the people there

invalid   someone who is weak because they are ill or injured

invent   to be the first person to think of a plan for a new machine or a better way of doing something

investigate   to try to find out as much as you can about something

invisible   not able to be seen
invisible ink

invitation   words that ask you politely to come
a party invitation

invite   to ask someone politely to come or do something

iris   **1** the coloured part of the eye
2 a plant with leaves shaped like swords and yellow, white, blue, or purple flowers

irises

iron   **1** a strong, heavy metal
2 a flat piece of metal with a handle. It is heated and used for making clothes smooth and flat.

ironmonger   someone who keeps a shop that sells tools, nails, and other metal things

irritable   easily annoyed
The child was tired and irritable.

irritate   to keep annoying someone
The buzzing fly irritated the horse.

Islam   a religion. People who believe in Islam call God "Allah".

island, isle   a piece of land with water all around it

italic   **1** a kind of writing
2 a kind of printing *like this*

itch   a feeling in your skin that makes you want to scratch yourself

item any one thing in a list or group of things
The first item on the shopping list is cheese.

itself **1** it and nothing else
The cat yawned and stretched itself.
2 *by itself* on its own
The robot can move by itself.

ivory **1** something that comes from the tusks of elephants. It is pale cream, hard, and very valuable.
2 the pale cream colour of ivory

ivy a climbing plant with shiny dark green leaves

J j

jab **1** to push roughly at something with your finger or the end of a stick
He jabbed the boy in the back to get his attention.
2 to stab something suddenly with the pointed part of a sharp tool
He jabbed his fork into the sausage.

jackdaw a black bird. Jackdaws sometimes steal bright things and hide them.

jacket a kind of short coat

jagged with sharp parts along the edge

jam **1** fruit boiled with sugar until it is thick
raspberry jam
2 a lot of people or cars crowded together so that it is difficult to move
a traffic jam
3 to become fixed and difficult to move
The door has jammed and I can't open it.

jar a container like the glass ones used for jam

jaw **1** the lower part of the face
2 one of the bones that hold the teeth

jealous unhappy because someone else seems to have more or be doing better than you
She was jealous of her sister's new bike.

jeans strong cotton trousers

jeep a very strong small car

jeer to make fun of someone because you think you are better than they are
The crowd jeered at the goalkeeper who had let in six goals.

jelly a sweet, shiny, slippery food that looks solid, though it melts in your mouth
orange jelly

jerk   to move suddenly or clumsily

jersey   something with sleeves that is knitted in wool and worn on the top half of the body

jet   1 a liquid or gas coming very quickly out of a small opening
They used a jet spray to paint the car.
2 an aeroplane with an engine that is driven by jets of hot gas

Jew   1 a person descended from the ancient tribes of Israel
2 a person who believes in Judaism

jewel   a valuable and beautiful stone

jewellery   necklaces, bracelets, rings, and brooches

jigsaw puzzle   a set of small pieces of cardboard or wood that fit together to make a picture

jingle   to make the sound tiny bells make

jockey   someone who rides horses in races

jog   1 to run slowly
2 to push against something
He jogged my elbow and I spilt the paint.

join   1 to put together to make one thing
Join the pieces of the jigsaw puzzle.
2 to become a member of a group
Join the Chess Club.

joiner   someone whose job is to make furniture and other things out of wood

joint   1 the place where two parts fit together. The ankle is the joint between the foot and the leg.
2 a large piece of meat

joke   something said or done to make people laugh

jolly   happy and cheerful

jolt   to shake suddenly
The passengers were jolted on the rough road.

jotter   a book where you can write things down quickly

journey   the travelling people do to get from one place to another place

joy   great happiness

Judaism   the religion of the Jewish people

judge   1 to decide whether something is good or bad, right or wrong, fair or unfair
2 someone who judges
The judge announced the results.

juggler   someone who entertains people by doing difficult throwing, catching, and balancing tricks

juice   the liquid in fruit and vegetables

jumble   a lot of different things all mixed up
a jumble sale

jump   to move up suddenly from the ground into the air

jumper   a jersey

junction a place where roads or railway lines meet

jungle a forest in a very hot, damp country

junior younger

junk **1** things that people do not want any more
2 a Chinese sailing boat

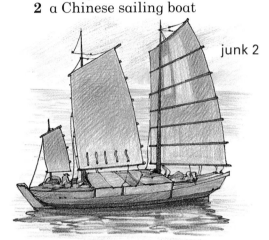
junk 2

just **1** fair to everyone
a just king
2 exactly
It's just what I wanted.
3 only
Just one more cake, please.

K k

kaleidoscope a thick tube you look through to see coloured patterns. The pattern changes when you turn the end of the tube.

kangaroo an Australian animal that jumps. Female kangaroos have pouches in which they carry their babies.

keel a long piece of wood or metal along the bottom of a boat
(See picture on p. 215)

keen very interested in something
keen on pop music

keep **1** to have something as your own and not get rid of it
He kept the money he found.
2 to make something stay as it is
Try to keep your clothes clean.
3 to look after something
She keeps rabbits.

kennel a little hut for keeping a dog in

kept see **keep**

kerb the blocks of stone along the edge of the pavement

kernel the part in the middle of a nut

kettle a metal container in which water is boiled. It has a lid, handle, and spout.

key **1** a piece of metal shaped so that it fits into a lock
2 a small lever pressed with the finger. Pianos and typewriters have keys.

keyboard the set of keys on a piano, a typewriter, or a computer

kid a young goat

kidnap to take someone away and keep them prisoner until you get what you want

kill to make someone or something die

kilogram a measure for weight
a kilogram of apples

kilometre a measure for length
1 kilometre = 1,000 metres

kilt a kind of pleated skirt worn by some Scotsmen

kind **1** ready to help and love other people
2 a sort
a special kind of paint

king a man who has been crowned as ruler of a country

kingdom   a land that is ruled by a king or queen

kingfisher   a brightly coloured bird that lives near water and catches fish

kiosk   **1** a telephone box
2 a small stall that sells newspapers, sweets, and tobacco

kipper   a dried fish that is ready to be cooked and eaten. Kippers have a strong taste.

kiss   to touch someone with your lips because you are fond of them

kitchen   the room where food is cooked

kite   a light frame covered in cloth or paper and flown in the wind at the end of a long piece of string

kitten   a very young cat

knee   the bony part in the middle of the leg where it bends

kneel   to get down on your knees
They knelt down and prayed.

knew   see **know**

knickers   pants worn by women and girls

knife   a tool with a long, sharp edge for cutting things
two knives

knight   **1** a man who has been given the title, Sir
Sir Francis Drake was a knight.
2 a man in armour who rode into battle on a horse

knit   to use wool and a pair of long needles to make clothes

knives   more than one **knife**

knob   the round handle on a door or drawer

knock   **1** to hit something hard
2 to hit something by accident
He knocked himself on the head.

knot   the twisted part where pieces of string, rope, cotton, or ribbon have been tied together

know   **1** to have something in your mind that you have found out
I knew all about it yesterday.
2 to have met someone before
I haven't known her long.

knowledge   things that are known and understood

known   see **know**

knuckle   one of the places where the fingers bend

koala   a furry Australian animal that looks like a small bear

koalas

Koran   the holy book of Islam that is read in all mosques

Ll

label a piece of card or sticky paper put on something to show what it is, whose it is, or where it is going

laboratory a room or building where scientific work is done

labour hard work

Labrador a kind of large black or light brown dog (See picture on p. 220)

lace 1 thin, pretty material with a pattern of holes in it. Lace is often used to decorate things.
2 a piece of thin cord used to tie up a shoe

lack to be without something
The team lacked a goalkeeper.

ladder two long bars with short bars between them that you can climb up or down

ladle a big, deep spoon used for serving soup

lady 1 a polite name for a woman
2 a title
Lady Jane Grey

ladybird a red or yellow insect with black spots on it that can fly

lag to be behind because you are moving too slowly
He's lagging behind again.

laid see **lay**

lain see **lie**

lair a wild animal's home

lake a large area of water with land all around it

lamb a young sheep

lame not able to walk properly

lamp something that gives light where you want it

lance a long spear like the ones used by knights long ago

land 1 all the dry parts of the earth's surface
2 to arrive by boat or aeroplane

landing the flat place at the top of the stairs in a building

landlady a woman who lets other people live in her house or flat in return for money

landlord a man who lets other people live in his house or flat in return for money

lane a narrow road

language words spoken or written by people
foreign languages

lantern a container for a light. It is made of metal and glass or something else that the light can shine through.

lap 1 the part from the waist to the knees of a person sitting down
2 once round a race course
3 to drink with the tongue, like a cat

larch a kind of tree. Larches have small cones and lose their leaves every winter.

lard white fat from pigs, used in cooking

larder a cool cupboard or small room where food is kept

large big

lark a small, brown bird that sings

lash 1 to tie tightly to something
2 to hit hard, usually with a whip

lasso (*say* la-soo)
a long rope with a loop at the end, tied so that the loop can get bigger or smaller. Cowboys use lassos for catching cattle.

last 1 after all the others
go out last
2 to go on for some time
The film lasted one hour.

latch a fastener on a gate or door

late 1 after the expected time
2 near the end of a day, month, or year
3 no longer alive
the late King

lather soap bubbles on the top of water

laugh to make sounds that show that you are happy or think something is very funny

laughter the sound of laughing

launch
1 a large boat with an engine
2 to push a boat into the water
They launched the lifeboat to rescue some people.
3 to send a spaceship from earth into space

launderette a place with washing-machines that people can pay to use

laundry
1 clothes that need to be washed
2 a place where people send dirty clothes and sheets to be washed

lavatory a toilet

lavender 1 a bush with pale purple flowers that smell very sweet
2 a pale purple colour

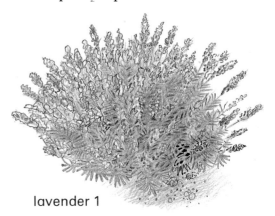

lavender 1

law a rule or set of rules that everyone in a country must keep

lawn the part of a garden that is covered with short grass

lay 1 to put something down
2 *to lay the table* to get the table ready for a meal
3 to make an egg
The hen laid two eggs today.
4 see **lie**

layer something flat that lies over or under another surface
a layer of icing on the cake

lazy   not willing to work

lead[1]   (*rhymes with* bed)
a soft, grey metal that is very heavy

lead[2]   (*rhymes with* seed)
1 to go in front of other people to show them where to go or what to do
He found us and led us to safety.
2 to be in charge of a group
You lead this team.
3 a strap fastened to a dog's collar so that you can control it
Keep your dog on its lead.

leader   a person or animal that leads

leaf   one of the flat green parts that grow on trees and other plants

league   a group of teams that play matches against each other

leak   to have a hole or crack that liquid or gas can get through

lean   **1** to bend your body towards something
I leant forward and looked.
2 to rest against something
Lean against me if you are tired.
3 to make something slope
Lean the ladder against the wall.
4 not fat
lean meat

leant   (*say* lent)
see **lean**

leap   to jump
I leapt up as if I'd been stung.

leapt   (*say* lept)
see **leap**

leap year   a year with an extra day in it, the 29th February. A leap year comes once every four years.

learn   **1** to find out about something
2 to find out how to do something
He learnt to swim last year.

leash   a dog's lead

least   **1** less than all the others
the least expensive bike
2 the smallest amount
The least you can do is say you are sorry.

leather   a strong material made from the skins of animals
leather shoes

leave   **1** to go from a person or place
2 to let something stay where it is
I've left my book at home.

leaves   more than one **leaf**

led   see **lead**[2]

ledge   a narrow shelf like the one that sticks out under a window

leek   a long, white vegetable with green leaves that tastes like an onion

leeks

left   **1** on the side opposite the right. Most people hold a fork in their left hand and a knife in their right hand.
2 see **leave**

left-handed   using the left hand to write and do other important things, because you find it easier than using the right hand

legend a story that was first told long ago by people who thought it was true. Most legends are not true.

leisure (*rhymes with* treasure) time when you can do what you want to do, because you do not have to work

lemon **1** a pale yellow fruit with a sour taste
2 the pale yellow colour of lemons

lemonade a drink made from lemons, sugar, and water

lend to let someone have something of yours for a short time
I lent you my bike yesterday.

length **1** how long something is
2 a piece of rope or cloth

lengthen **1** to make longer
You can lengthen a rubber band by stretching it.
2 to get longer
The days lengthen in March.

lens a curved piece of glass or plastic that makes light go where it is needed. Spectacles, cameras, and telescopes have lenses.

lent see **lend**

leopard a big wild cat found in Africa and Asia. It has yellow fur with black spots on it.

leotard (*say* lee-a-tard) a piece of clothing worn by acrobats and dancers

less **1** not as much
2 take away. Six less four is two, $6 - 4 = 2$.

lessen **1** to make less
Take out some shopping and it will lessen the weight of the bag.
2 to become less

lesson **1** the time when someone is teaching you
2 something that you have to learn
Road safety is an important lesson for everyone.

letter **1** one of the signs used for writing words, such as a, b, or c
2 a written message sent to another person

lettuce a vegetable with green leaves that are eaten in salads

level **1** flat and smooth
level ground
2 equal
Your scores are level.

lever a bar that is pulled down to lift something heavy or make a machine work

liable **1** likely to do or get something
2 responsible for something

liar someone who tells lies

library a building or room where a lot of books are kept for people to use

licence a printed paper that says that you can do, own, or use something
a dog licence

lick to move the tongue over something

lie 1 to rest with the body flat as it is in bed
I lay down and went to sleep.
The cat has lain here all night.
He has been lying here.
2 to say something that is not true
You lied to me yesterday.
He was lying.
3 something you say that is not true
He tells lies.

life the time between birth and death
Do cats have nine lives?

lifeboat a boat that goes out to sea in bad weather to save peoples' lives

lift 1 to move upwards
Lift out the shopping from the trolley.
2 to pick up something
Can you lift this heavy box?
3 a machine for taking people or things up and down inside a building
4 a ride in someone's car or lorry

light 1 the power that makes things able to be seen. Light comes from the sun, the stars, flames, and lamps.
2 to start something burning
I struck a match and lit the fire.
3 pale
light blue
4 weighing little
as light as a feather

lighten 1 to make lighter
We need to lighten the ship's cargo.
2 to get lighter
The sky lightened as the sun rose.

lighthouse a tower with a bright light that warns ships of rocks or other dangers

lightning the bright light that flashes in the sky during a thunderstorm

like 1 to think someone or something is pleasant
2 nearly the same as another person or thing

likely expected to happen or to be true
He is the likely winner of the race as he has trained hard.

lilac 1 a tree with a lot of white or pale purple flowers that smell very sweet
2 a pale purple colour

lily a beautiful white flower grown in gardens (See picture on p. 218)

limb a leg, arm, or wing

lime **1** a white powder used in making cement
2 a pale green fruit like a lemon
3 a kind of tree

limit a line or point that people cannot or should not pass
a speed limit

limp **1** walk with difficulty because there is something wrong with your leg or foot
2 not stiff
The cardboard box became limp and soggy in the rain.

line **1** a long, thin mark like this
—————————————
2 a row of people or things
3 the set of metal rails a train moves along

linen strong cloth used for making sheets and table-cloths

liner a big ship for taking people on long journeys

linger to be slow to leave
After the concert they lingered outside hoping to meet one of the band.

lining cloth covering the inside of clothes or curtains

link **1** to join things together
2 one of the rings in a chain

lino, linoleum a stiff, shiny covering for the floor

lint soft material for putting on an injured part of the body

lion a large, light brown wild cat found in Africa and India

lioness a female lion

lipstick something that looks like a crayon and is used for colouring lips

liquid anything that is like water, oil, or milk

liquorice a black sweet that you get in sticks and other shapes

list a group of things or names written down one after the other
a shopping list

listen to pay attention in order to hear something

lit see **light**

litre (*rhymes with* Peter)
a measure for liquid
a litre of paint

litter **1** paper, empty packets, bottles, and other rubbish, dropped or left lying about
2 all the young animals born to the same mother at the same time
The cat had a litter of seven kittens.

little **1** not big
a little boy
2 not much
little time

live[1] (*rhymes with* give)
1 to have your life
2 to have your home in a place

live[2] (*rhymes with* dive)
alive
Careful! This electricity wire is live.

lively full of life and energy
a lively dance, a lively horse

lives (*rhymes with* dives)
more than one **life**

lizard a creature with skin like a snake and which has four legs

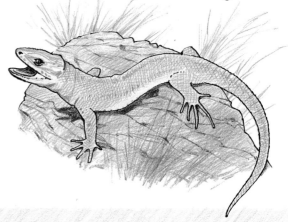

load 1 something that is carried
The lorry was carrying a heavy load.
2 to put things on to something that will carry them
Load the suitcases into the car boot.
3 to put bullets into a gun
Load the gun.

loaf bread in the shape it was baked in
two loaves

loan anything that is lent to someone

loaves more than one **loaf**

lobster a sea creature with a shell, two large claws, eight legs, and a tail

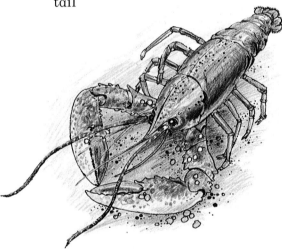

local belonging to one place
local radio

loch a lake in Scotland

lock 1 to fasten with a key
Turn the key to lock the door.
2 a fastening for a door, gate, or box that is opened with a key
The key is stuck in the lock.
3 a piece of hair
She cut her golden locks.

locomotive the engine that pulls a train

locust an insect that flies about in a large group, destroying plants by eating them

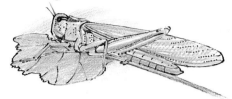

lodge 1 to pay to live in someone else's house
2 a small house near the gates of a large garden that belongs to a much bigger house

lodger someone who pays to live in another person's home

loft a room in the roof, where things can be kept

loiter to stand about with nothing to do

loll to sit or lie in an untidy, lazy way

lollipop a big sweet on the end of a stick

lonely 1 sad because you are on your own
2 far from others
a lonely house

long 1 measuring a lot from one end to the other
a long road
2 taking a lot of time
a long holiday
3 *to long for* to want something very much

look 1 to use your eyes
2 *to look for* to try to find something
3 to seem
You look sad.

loom a machine for weaving cloth

loop a ring made in rope, wire, thread, or ribbon

loose (*say* loos)
1 not tight
His baby tooth was loose.
2 not fixed to anything
The dog is loose – he has shaken off his lead.

loosen **1** to make looser
He loosened his tie.
2 to get looser
The opening and closing of the door has loosened the screw.

loot things that have been stolen
The pirates hid the loot in the sand.

lord **1** a nobleman
2 a title
Lord Baden-Powell

lorry a big, open truck for taking heavy things by road

lose (*say* looz)
1 to be without something you once had
2 to be without something, because you cannot find it
I've lost my coat.
3 to be beaten in a game
We lost last Saturday's match.

lost see **lose**

lotion a liquid that is put on the skin

loud **1** very easy to hear
2 noisy

loudspeaker **1** a machine that makes sound louder
2 the part of a television, radio, or record-player that the sound comes from

lounge a room with comfortable chairs in it

love to like very much

lovely **1** beautiful
a lovely face
2 pleasing
a lovely idea

low not high

loyal always true to your friends

luck the way things happen that have not been planned

lucky having good luck
a lucky charm

luggage bags, boxes, and suitcases taken by someone on a journey

lukewarm only just warm

lullaby a song that is sung to send a baby to sleep

lumber **1** rough wood
2 to move in a clumsy way

lump **1** a solid thing with no clear shape
a lump of clay
2 a swelling

lunch a meal eaten in the middle of the day

lung one of the two parts inside the body used for breathing

lurch to lean suddenly to one side
The train lurched and the passengers were thrown about.

lurk to wait where you cannot be seen
The boy lurked in the bushes hoping to surprise his friends.

luxury   something expensive that you like very much but do not really need

lying   see **lie**

M m

mac   short for **mackintosh**

machine   something with several parts that work together to do a job
a washing-machine

machine-gun   a gun that can keep firing very quickly for a long time

machinery   machines

mackintosh   a raincoat

madam   a word sometimes used when speaking politely to a woman, instead of her name

made   see **make**

magazine   a kind of thin book that comes out every week or month with different stories and pictures in it

maggot   a tiny worm that comes from an egg laid by a fly

magic   the power to do wonderful things or clever tricks that people cannot usually do

magician   someone who knows a lot about magic and uses it

magnet   a metal bar that can make pieces of iron or steel come and stick to it

magnificent   **1** very grand
a magnificent palace
2 splendid
a magnificent present

magnify   to make something look bigger
a magnifying glass

magpie   a black and white bird. Magpies sometimes steal bright things and hide them.

maid   a girl or woman who is a servant

mail   letters, cards, and parcels sent through the post

main   the most important
a main road

majesty   a word used when speaking to a king or queen
Your Majesty

make   **1** to get something new by putting other things together
I've made a boat out of paper and wood.
2 to cause something to happen
You made me do this last time.

make-up   cream, lipstick, and powder put on the face to make it look different

male   any person or animal that can become a father. Men, boys, stags, and bulls are all males.

mammal   any animal that has hair and can feed its babies with its own milk
Whales, lions, and people are all mammals.

man   a fully grown male
two men

manage   **1** to be in charge of a shop or factory
Her job was to manage the factory.
2 to be able to do something although it is difficult
After a chase they managed to catch the rabbit.

mane   the long hair along a horse's back or on a lion's head and neck

manger   a long, narrow container that horses and cattle can eat from when they are in the stable

mangle   to cut up or crush something roughly

manner   the way something happens or is done

manners   your behaviour towards other people
She taught her children to have good manners.

manor   a big, important house in the country

mansion   a big, important house

mantelpiece   the shelf above a fire-place

manufacture   to make large numbers of the same thing

many   a large number of people or things

map   a diagram that shows parts of the world and where different places are

marble   **1** a small, glass ball used in some games
2 a kind of smooth stone used for building or making statues

march   to walk like soldiers on parade

mare   a female horse

margarine   a food that looks and tastes like butter, but is not made from milk

margin   the empty space in a book between the edge of a page and the writing or pictures

marigold   a bright orange or yellow flower grown in gardens

mark   **1** a stain, spot, or line that spoils something
dirty marks
2 a sign or number put on a piece of work to show how good it is

market   a group of stalls selling food and other things. Markets are usually held in the open air.

marmalade   jam made from oranges or lemons

maroon   **1** a very dark red colour
2 to leave someone in a wild and lonely place without any way of escaping from it
After the shipwreck he was marooned on an island.

marriage   a wedding

marry   to become someone's husband or wife

marsh   a piece of very wet ground

marvellous   wonderful
a marvellous story

marzipan   a sweet food made from almonds

mash   to crush something to make it soft and get rid of the lumps
mashed potato

mask   a covering worn on the face to protect or hide it

masks

mass   **1** a large number or amount
2 A Roman Catholic church service

massive   very big

mast   a tall pole that holds up a ship's sails, a flag, or an aerial (See picture on p. 215)

master   a man who is in charge

match   **1** a small, thin stick that gives a flame when rubbed on something rough
2 a game played between two sides
3 to be the same as another thing or like it in some way
In some card games you have to find the matching pictures.

material   **1** anything used for making something else
Cement and bricks are building materials.
2 wool, cotton, or anything else that is woven and used for making clothes or covers

mathematics, maths   finding out about numbers, measurement, and shapes

matter   **1** to be important
Does it matter if I arrive late?
2 something you need to think about or do
a serious matter
3 *What's the matter?* What is wrong?

mattress   the thick, soft part of a bed

may   **1** can
May I go out to play?
2 will perhaps
It may rain later.
It might rain later.

mayor   the person in charge of the council in a town or city

maze   a set of lines or paths that twist and turn so much that it is very easy to lose the way

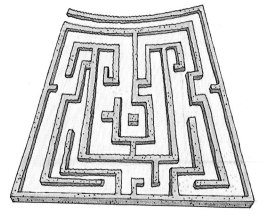

meadow   a field covered with grass

meal   the food eaten at breakfast, lunch, dinner, tea, or supper

mean **1** not generous
She's mean – she never shares her sweets.
2 to plan in your mind
I meant to tell him, but I forgot.
3 to have a meaning
This dictionary tells you what words mean.

meaning what someone wants to say with the words they are using
The angry farmer's meaning was clear: we must keep off his land.

meant (*rhymes with* tent)
see **mean**

meanwhile during the time something else is happening
You set the table. Meanwhile I'll prepare the lunch.

measles an illness that makes red spots come on the skin

measure **1** to find out how big something is
2 a unit used for measuring. Kilograms, grams, pounds, and ounces are all measures for weight.

measurement how much something measures

meat the flesh of animals used as food

mechanical worked by or like machinery
a mechanical digger

medal a piece of metal in the shape of a coin, star, or cross given to someone very brave or very good at something
a gold medal

medallist someone who has won a medal

meddle to take part in something that has nothing to do with you
Don't meddle in their quarrel.

medicine liquid or tablets that a sick person has to swallow in order to get better again

medium of middle size

meek gentle and not proud

meet **1** to come together
2 to come face to face with another person
I met her in town yesterday.

meeting a group of people who have come together to talk about something or to listen to someone

melon a large, juicy fruit with a yellow or green skin

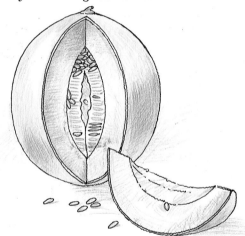

melt to change into a liquid when heated. Ice melts.

member someone who belongs to a group

memory **1** the ability to remember
2 anything that is remembered
The old man had happy memories of when he was a boy.
3 the part of a computer that stores information

men more than one **man**

menagerie a kind of small zoo

mend to make a damaged thing as useful as it was before

mention   to speak of something or someone when you are talking about other things
He was talking about the zoo and she mentioned that she liked animals.

menu   a list of the different kinds of food you can choose for your meal

mercy   being kind to someone instead of punishing them
Show mercy to the prisoners.

meringue   (*say* me-<u>rang</u>)
a crisp cake made from the whites of eggs mixed with sugar and then baked

mermaid   a creature in stories, that looks like a woman but has a fish's tail instead of legs

merry   happy and gay

mess   things that are untidy, dirty, or mixed up

message   words that you send to someone to tell them something when you cannot speak to them yourself

messenger   someone who takes a message to someone else

met   see **meet**

metal   something hard that melts when it is very hot. Gold, silver, iron, and tin are all kinds of metal.

meteor   a small piece of rock or metal that moves through space and burns up when it gets near the earth

meteorite   a lump of rock or metal that has fallen through space and landed on the earth

meter   a machine that measures how much of something has been used
gas meters

method   the way you choose to do something
His method of adding numbers was very strange.

metre   a measure for length
1,000 metres = 1 kilometre

metric system   a way of measuring things. The metric system uses metres for measuring length, kilograms for measuring weight and litres for measuring liquids.

mew, miaow   (*say* mee-<u>ow</u>)
to make the cry a cat makes

mice   more than one **mouse**

microchip   one of the tiny pieces used to make a computer

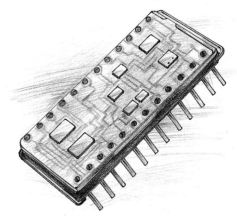

microcomputer the kind of computer people might use in their homes or on their desks at work

microphone a machine that changes sound into electricity so that it can be sent along wires to loudspeakers, telephones, or aerials

microscope an instrument that makes it possible to see very tiny things by making them look much bigger

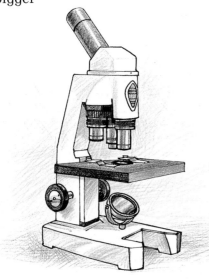

microwave oven an electronic oven that cooks food very quickly

midday twelve o'clock in the day

middle the part of something that is the same distance from all its sides or edges or from both its ends

midnight twelve o'clock at night

might see **may**

mild gentle

mile a measure for length

milk a white liquid that mothers and some female animals feed their babies with. People can drink cows' milk.

mill **1** a place with machinery for making corn into flour
2 a kind of factory
A paper mill makes paper from wood.

millionaire someone who owns a million pounds

mime to tell someone something by using actions not words

mimic to copy someone's voice in order to make fun of them

mince meat cut into very small pieces

mincemeat a sweet mixture of chopped fruit and other things, cooked inside pastry at Christmas

mind **1** the power to think, feel, and understand
2 to look after
I'll mind the baby.
3 *Mind out!* Be careful!
4 to be worried or upset by something
Do you mind missing the party?

mine **1** a place where people work to dig coal, metal, jewels, or salt out of the ground
2 a bomb hidden in the ground or the sea to blow up things that come close to it
3 belonging to me
That's mine.

miner someone who works down a mine

mineral **1** any useful or valuable rock people get out of the ground
2 a cold drink with a lot of tiny bubbles in it

mingle to mix

miniature tiny, but just like something much bigger

minister someone who serves God by being in charge of a church

minnow   a tiny fish found in rivers, streams, lakes, and ponds

minstrel   a man who sang or played music to entertain people long ago

mint   **1** a green plant used in cooking to give food a better flavour
2 a sweet that tastes of mint
a peppermint
3 a place where coins are made

minus   take away. Six minus two is four, 6 − 2 = 4.

minute¹   (*say* <u>min</u>-it)
sixty seconds

minute²   (*say* my-<u>newt</u>)
very tiny

miracle   something wonderful that has happened, although it did not seem possible

mirage
a trick of the light that makes people see things that are not really there, such as pools of water in deserts

mirror   a piece of glass, in which you can see yourself

misbehave   to be naughty

mischief   silly or bad behaviour that gets you into trouble

mischievous   likely to do silly or naughty things
The mischievous puppy pulled the washing from the line.

miser   someone who has a lot of money, but tries to spend as little as possible so that they can keep it

miserable   very unhappy

misery   suffering
great misery

misfortune   something unlucky that happens

miss   **1** to fail to hit, catch, see, hear, or find something
2 to be sad because someone is no longer with you

mission   an important job that someone is sent away to do

mist   damp air that it is difficult to see through

mistake   something you have done or thought that is wrong
spelling mistakes

mistletoe   a plant which grows on other trees. It is used to decorate houses at Christmas.

misunderstand   to get the wrong idea about something
You misunderstood what I said.

mitten   a kind of glove with two parts, one for the thumb and one for all the fingers

mix   to stir or shake different things together to make one thing

mixture   something made of different things mixed together

moan   **1** to make a soft sound that shows you are in pain or trouble
The boy moaned as they lifted him into the ambulance.
2 to grumble
The class moaned about missing the swimming lesson.

moat   a ditch dug round a castle and usually filled with water

mock   **1** to make fun of someone
2 not real
a mock battle

model   **1** a small copy of something
He made a model aeroplane.
2 someone whose job is to wear new clothes to show people what they look like
The model wore the latest fashions.

modern   of the kind that is usual now
a modern house

moist   damp

mole   a small, grey, furry animal that digs holes under the ground

moment   a very small amount of time

monarch   a ruler who is a king, queen, emperor, or empress

monastery   a house where monks live and work

money   the coins and pieces of paper used when people buy and sell things

mongrel   a dog that is a mixture of different kinds of dog

monitor   a boy or girl with a special job to do at school

monk   one of a group of men who live together and obey rules because of the religion they believe in

monkey   an animal with hands, feet it can use like hands, long arms, and a tail

monster   a large, frightening animal in stories

month   a measure for time. There are twelve months in a year.

monument   a statue or building made so that people will remember someone or something

mood   the way you feel
in a good mood

moon   the planet that goes round the earth and shines in the sky at night. Sometimes it looks completely round and sometimes like part of a circle.

moor   **1** an area of land that has bushes but no trees, because it is too windy
2 to tie up a boat so that it will not float away

more   **1** a larger number or amount
2 again
I'll tell you once more.

morning   the time from the beginning of the day until the middle of the day

mortar   a mixture of sand, cement, and water, used in building to stick bricks together

mosaic   a picture made from coloured pieces of paper, glass, stone, or wood

moss   a plant that grows in damp places and has no flower
(See picture on p. 218)

mosque   a building where Muslims worship

most   **1** more than any other
2 very
She was most kind.

moth   an insect with large, coloured wings. Moths usually fly around at night.

moths

mother   a female parent

motor   the part inside a car or machine that makes it move

motor bike, motor cycle   a kind of bicycle with an engine but with no pedals

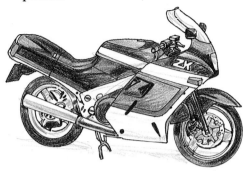

mould   (*rhymes with* old)
1 a kind of fungus. It is the furry stuff that sometimes grows on food that has gone bad.
2 a container for making things like jelly or plaster set in the shape that is wanted

mound   a pile of earth

mount   to get on to a horse or bicycle so that you can ride it

mountain   a very high hill

mouse   a very small animal with a long tail and a pointed nose
three blind mice

moustache   hair that grows above a man's top lip

mouth   the part of the face that opens for eating and speaking

move   **1** to take from one place to another
2 to go from one place to another

movement   moving
a sudden movement

mow   to cut grass

much   a lot of something

mud   wet soil

muddle   to mix things up and make a mess of something

muesli a food made of cereals, nuts, and dried fruit

mule an animal that is half horse and half donkey

multiply to make something a number of times bigger. Two multiplied by four is eight:
$2 \times 4 = 8$.

mumble to speak in a way that is not clear so that it is difficult to hear your words

mumps an illness that makes the sides of the face swell

munch to chew noisily

murder to kill someone on purpose

murmur to speak in a very soft, low voice

muscle one of the parts inside the body that become tight or loose in order to make the body move

museum a place where a lot of interesting things are kept for people to go and see

mushroom a kind of fungus that people can eat

music the sounds made by someone singing or playing a musical instrument

musical 1 having to do with music
musical instruments
2 good at music

Muslim someone who believes in the religion of Islam

mussel a small sea creature that lives inside a pair of black shells

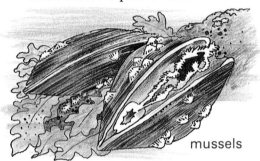

mussels

must have to
I must go now.

mustard 1 a yellow powder or paste used to give food a strong flavour
2 *mustard and cress* small green plants eaten in salads

mutiny an attack made by soldiers or sailors against the officers in charge of them

mutter to murmur or grumble
'Why does it always have to be me?' he muttered to himself.

mutton meat from a sheep

muzzle 1 an animal's nose and mouth
2 a cover put over an animal's nose and mouth so that it cannot bite

myself 1 I and no one else
2 *by myself* on my own

mysterious strange and puzzling

mystery something strange and puzzling that has happened

N n

nag to keep telling someone that you are not pleased and that they ought to behave differently
She nagged him to tidy his room.

nail **1** the hard part that covers the end of each finger and toe
2 a small piece of metal with a sharp point, used for fastening pieces of wood together

naked (*say* nay-kid)
without any clothes or covering

name what you call someone or something

nanny **1** someone who looks after young children
2 a grandmother

nanny-goat a female goat

nappy a piece of cloth put round a baby's bottom

narrow not wide

nasty **1** not pleasant
a nasty day
2 very dirty
a nasty mess
3 not kind
a nasty person

nation a country and the people who live in it

national belonging to one country

native someone born in the place that you are thinking of
a native of Scotland

natural **1** made by nature, not by people or machines
2 normal
It is natural for birds to fly.

nature **1** plants, animals, the sea, and everything else in the world that was not made by people
2 what a person or animal is really like
My dog has a very gentle nature.

naughty badly behaved

navigate to make sure that a ship, aeroplane, or car is going in the right direction

navy **1** a group of ships and the people trained to use them for fighting
2 dark blue

near not far away

nearly not quite
nearly 3 o'clock, nearly £100, nearly there

neat tidy

necessary needed very much
It is necessary to water plants in hot weather.

neck the part of the body that joins the head to the shoulders

necklace beads, jewels, or a chain worn round the neck

nectar a sweet liquid inside flowers. Bees collect nectar to make honey.

need **1** to be without something that you ought to have
2 to have to do something
I need to go to the dentist.

needle **1** a very thin, pointed piece of metal. Needles used for sewing have holes in them.
2 one of a pair of rods used for knitting
3 a very thin, pointed leaf. Pine trees have needles.

neglect to leave something alone and not look after it
He neglected the garden and it was full of weeds.

neigh to make the noise a horse makes

neighbour someone who lives next door or near to you

neither not either
Neither of the twins has a bike.

nephew the son of a brother or sister

nerve **1** one of the small parts inside the body that carry messages to and from the brain, so that the body can feel and move **2** brave or calm behaviour when there is danger
Don't lose your nerve.

nervous **1** afraid and excited because of something you have to do
She was nervous before the start of the school play.
2 easily frightened
a nervous animal

nest a cosy place made by birds, mice, and some other animals for their babies

nestle to curl up comfortably
He nestled down in bed.

netball a ball game played outside between two teams of girls. The ball has to be thrown into a net on a tall post.

nettle a plant with its stem and leaves covered in hairs that sting (See picture on p. 218)

never not ever

new **1** just bought or made
a new bike
2 different
my new school

news words that tell you about something that has just happened

newspaper large sheets of paper folded together, with the news printed on them. Most newspapers come out every day.

newt a small creature that lives near water and has four legs and a long tail

next the nearest

nib the pointed metal part at the end of the kind of pen that needs ink

nibble to eat something by biting off a little at a time. Rabbits nibble carrots.

nice pleasant

nickname a name you call someone instead of his real name. William Cody's nickname was Buffalo Bill.

niece the daughter of a brother or sister

night the time when it is dark

nightingale a small, brown bird that sings at night

nightmare   a frightening dream

nimble   able to move quickly and easily
Her nimble fingers sewed the tiny stitches.

nip   to bite someone or squeeze their skin between the thumb and finger

nitwit   someone who is very silly

noble   brave and generous

nobleman   a man who is a duke or lord

nobody   no person

noise   sound that is loud and often not pleasant

none   not any or not one

nonsense   something that does not mean anything

noon   twelve o'clock in the day

no one   no person

noose   a loop made in a piece of rope so that when the rope is pulled the loop gets smaller

normal   usual or ordinary
The normal time for school to start is 9 o'clock.

north   the direction to your left when you face east

northern   from the north or in the north

nose   the part of the face that is used for breathing and smelling

nostril   one of the two holes at the end of the nose for taking in air

notch   a mark like a V, cut into something

note   **1** a short letter
2 one sound in music
Play a note on the piano.

nothing   not anything

notice   **1** to see something and think about it
She noticed the milk bottles were still on the doorstep.
2 something fixed to a wall or a piece of board, for you to read
Please read the notice-board.

nought   the sign for nothing, 0

noun   any word that tells you what someone or something is called.
Air, Ann, speed, England, and *chair* are all nouns.

nourish   to feed someone well

novelty   something new or unusual

now   at this time

nowhere   not anywhere

nozzle   the part at the end of a piece of pipe where a spray of liquid or powder comes out

nude   without any clothes

nudge   to push someone with your elbow to make them notice something

nugget   a lump of gold

nuisance   someone or something that causes trouble
It's a nuisance that we missed the bus.

numb   not able to feel anything

number   the word or sign that tells you how many. 1, 2, and 3 are numbers.

numerous   many

nun   one of a group of women who live together and obey rules because of the religion they believe in

nurse   someone whose job is to look after people who are ill or hurt

nursery   a place where very young children go to play and be looked after

nut   **1** a kind of fruit that you chew after you have taken off its hard shell
walnut, peanut
2 a short piece of metal that is screwed on to the end of a bolt to make it firmer

nutmeg   a hard seed that is made into a powder and used in cooking to give food a better flavour

nylon   a very strong thin material for making clothes and other things

O o —————————————

oak   a large tree with seeds called acorns (See picture on p. 219)

oar   a long pole with a flat part at one end, used for rowing a boat

oasis   a place in a desert with water and trees

oath   a serious promise made to God

oats   a plant grown by farmers. Its seed is used for feeding animals and for making food such as porridge. (See picture on p. 218)

obedient   willing to do what you are told to do
His dog is always very obedient.

obey   to do what you are told to do

object[1]   (*say* <u>ob</u>-ject)
anything that can be seen or touched

object[2]   (*say* ob-<u>ject</u>)
to say that you do not like or agree with something

oblong   the shape of a door or this page
(See the list of shapes on p. 223)

observe   **1** to watch carefully
We observed the robin building her nest.
2 to say something that you have noticed

obstacle   something that is in the way

obstinate   not willing to change your ideas even though they might be wrong

obstruct   to be in the way so that something cannot get past
A fallen tree was obstructing the road.

obtain   to get

obvious   very easy to see or understand
The answer to the problem was obvious.

occasion   the time when something happens
a special occasion

occasionally   sometimes

occupation   any job or hobby

occupy   **1** to live in something
2 to keep someone busy and interested
Keeping young children occupied is a hard job.

occur   **1** to happen
   2 to come into your mind
   An idea occurred to me.

ocean   a big sea

o'clock   by the clock
   one o'clock

octopus   a sea creature with eight
arms

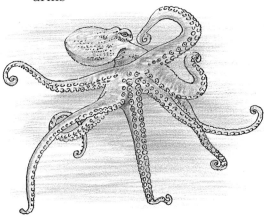

odd   **1** strange
   an odd person
   2 not even
   Five is an odd number.
   3 not alike
   odd shoes

odour   a smell

off   **1** away
   They ran off.
   2 not on
   Turn the tap off.

offend   to hurt someone's feelings

offensive   nasty and very annoying
an offensive smell

offer   **1** to hold out something so
that another person can take it if
they want it
   2 to say that you are willing to do
something
He offered to tidy the classroom.

office   a room with desks and
telephones, where people work

officer   someone in the army, navy,
or air force, who is in charge of
others

often   many times

ogre   (*say* o-ger)
a giant in stories who eats people

oil   a thick, slippery liquid. Oil is put
in machines to make them work
better and is burnt to make heat.
Another kind of oil is used in
cooking.

ointment   a cream for putting on
sore skin or cuts

old   **1** born or made a long time ago
   *He's an old man. He's nearly
ninety.*
   2 not new
   *It's an old car. We've had it ten
years.*

old-fashioned   of the kind that was
usual a long time ago
old-fashioned clothes

omelette   eggs that are mixed
together and fried

omit   to leave out
*She omitted the first story and just
read the second one.*

once   **1** one time
   *She only missed school once that
term.*
   2 at one time
   Once dinosaurs roamed the earth.

onion   a round, white vegetable
with a very strong flavour

only   **1** no more than
   only two cakes
   2 one by itself
   the only one left

ooze   to come slowly through a hole
or small opening. Blood oozes from
small cuts.
*Toothpaste was oozing through a
hole in the tube.*

open 1 not closed
2 to make open

opera a play in which all or most of the words are sung

operation 1 something done by doctors to a sick person's body to make it healthy again
2 the working of a machine

opinion what you think of something

opportunity a good chance to do something

opposite 1 facing
The house on the opposite side of the road is for sale.
2 something that is as different as possible from another thing. Hot is the opposite of cold.

optician someone who makes or sells spectacles

orange 1 a round, juicy fruit with thick peel and white pips
2 the colour of this fruit

orbit the path in space of something moving round the sun or a planet. The moon is in orbit round the earth.

orchard a place where a lot of fruit trees grow

orchestra a large group of people playing musical instruments together

ordeal a time when you have to put up with great pain or trouble

order 1 to tell someone to do something
The officer ordered the soldiers to march.
2 to ask for something to be brought to you
He ordered fish and chips in the café.
3 *in order* properly arranged

ordinary not special in any way

ore a piece of rock with metal in it

organ a large musical instrument like a piano, with pedals and pipes

organize 1 to get people working together to do something
2 to plan and arrange things like parties, concerts, or holidays
She is good at organizing things.

original 1 made first, before any others
2 new and not copied from anywhere
an original idea

ornament something put in a place to make it look pretty

orphan a child whose mother and father are dead

ostrich a very large bird that cannot fly and has long legs

other not the same as this
The other sweets were better.

otherwise or else

otter   a furry animal that lives near water. Otters have long tails.

ought   should
I ought to go now.

ounce   a measure for weight

ourselves   **1** we and no one else
We tidied the room ourselves.
2 *by ourselves* on our own

out   **1** not in
2 not burning
The fire has gone out.

outcast   someone ignored and left by their family and friends

outfit   clothes that are worn together
a Brownie outfit

outing   a day or afternoon out somewhere
an outing to the zoo

outlaw   someone long ago who had to hide, because, as a punishment they were not protected by the law and anyone could kill them. Robin Hood was a famous outlaw.

outline   a line round the edge of something, that shows its shape

outside   **1** not inside
2 the surface or edges of something

outskirts   the parts on the outside of an area or town

outstanding   unusually good
outstanding work

oval   the shape of an egg
(See the list of shapes on p. 223)

oven   the space inside a stove, where food can be baked or roasted

over   **1** above or covering
He pulled his hood over his head.
2 finished
Playtime is over.
3 left
Is there any food left over?
4 more than
There were over 40,000 at the match.

overall   including everything

overalls   something worn over other clothes to keep them clean

overboard   over the side of a boat into the water
Man overboard!

overflow   to come over the sides of a container, because there is too much in it

overhead   **1** above the head
overhead wires
2 in the sky above
a plane flying overhead

overtake   to catch up and pass someone

overturn   to push or knock something over

owe   to have to pay money to someone

owl   a bird with large eyes that hunts smaller animals at night

own **1** to have something that belongs to you
2 *to own up* to say that you were the one who did something
3 *my own* mine and no one else's
4 *on my own* by myself

ox a large animal kept for its meat or for pulling carts
two oxen

oxygen the gas in the air that everyone needs to breathe in order to stay alive

oyster a sea creature that lives inside a pair of shells

P p

pace **1** one step
2 how quickly something happens or moves

pack **1** to put things into a box, bag, or suitcase in order to move them or store them
2 a group of dogs or other animals
a pack of wolves
3 a group of Brownies or Cubs
4 a set of cards used in games

package a parcel

packet a small parcel

pad **1** sheets of writing paper joined together along one edge so that you can tear a sheet off when you need it
2 soft material folded up into a kind of cushion to protect something
shin-pads
3 to walk softly

paddle **1** to walk about in shallow water
I like paddling.
2 a thin piece of wood with a flat part at the end, used to make a canoe move

padlock a lock joined to something by a metal loop

padlock

page **1** one side of a piece of paper that is part of a book
2 a little boy who walks behind the bride at a wedding

paid see **pay**

pail a bucket

pain the feeling you have when part of your body is injured or sick

paint **1** a coloured liquid put on the surface of something to colour it
We bought a tin of paint.
2 to use paint to colour something
Paint the door blue.

painting a picture that has been painted

pair two people, animals, or things that belong together
a pair of gloves

palace a very large house where a king, queen, or some other very important person lives

pale **1** almost white
a pale face
2 light
a pale blue sky

palette a piece of board on which artists mix their colours while they are painting

paling a wooden fence

palm **1** the inside of the hand between the fingers and wrist
2 a tropical tree with large leaves and no branches

pamper to treat a person or animal too well

pancake flour, milk, and egg mixed together and fried

panda an animal found in China. Giant pandas look like large black and white bears.

pane a piece of glass in a window

panel a long, flat piece of wood or metal that is part of a door, wall, or piece of furniture

panic sudden fear that cannot be controlled

pansy a small plant with a brightly coloured flower (See picture on p. 218)

pant to take the short, quick breaths you take after running

panther an Indian leopard

pantomime a kind of play, usually done at Christmas. It tells a fairy story and has singers and comedians in it.

pantry a small room where food is kept

pants **1** underpants
2 trousers

paper **1** wet rags, straw, or tiny pieces of wood pressed and dried into very thin sheets. Paper is used for making books and wrapping up things.
2 a newspaper

parable a story told to teach people something

parachute a large piece of cloth that opens up like an umbrella when a cord is pulled. It is tied to someone's back so that they can jump out of an aeroplane and float safely down to the ground.

parade people marching along, while other people watch them

paraffin a liquid made from oil, that is burnt to make heat

parallel lines straight lines that are always the same distance from each other

paralysed not able to move or feel anything

parcel something wrapped up ready to be carried or posted

pardon to forgive

parent   1 a person who has a child
2 an animal that has young ones

parish   an area that has its own church and priest or minister. Some parishes have their own schools.

park   1 a large garden where anyone can walk or play
2 to leave a car somewhere for a time until it is needed again

parliament   the group of people that makes the laws of a country

parrot   a brightly coloured bird that can learn to repeat things that are said to it

parrots

parsley   a green plant used in cooking to give a stronger flavour to food

parsnip   a pale yellow vegetable with a sweet taste

part   anything that belongs to something bigger

particle   a very tiny piece
particles of dust

particular   only this one and no other

partner   one of a pair of people who dance together or play on the same side in a game

party   a group of people enjoying themselves together
a Christmas party

pass   1 to go by
On my way to school I pass the shop.
2 to give someone something they want, but cannot reach themselves
Please pass the salt.
3 to be successful in a test
She's passed her driving test.

passage   a corridor

passenger   anyone travelling in a bus, train, ship, or aeroplane, except the driver and crew

Passover   a holy time for Jews

passport   special papers printed by the government that a person has to have with them in order to go to another country

past   1 the time that has gone
In the past people used horses to travel.
2 up to and further than something
Go past the school.

pasta   (*say* pass-ta)
a food made from flour and water. Spaghetti is one kind of pasta, but there are many other shapes and sizes.

paste   a wet mixture used for sticking paper to things

pastime   something you do or play in your free time
Her favourite pastime is watching television.

pastry   a mixture of flour, fat, and water rolled flat and baked

pasture   land covered in grass that cattle, sheep, or horses can eat

patch   1 a small piece of material put over something to mend it or protect it
2 a small piece of ground
They have a vegetable patch.

path   a very narrow way that you can go along to get somewhere

patience   the ability to be patient

patient   **1** someone who is ill and being looked after by a doctor
The patient lay in the hospital bed.
2 able to bear pain or able to wait for a long time without getting angry
They sat in the queue patiently.

patrol   a group of soldiers or policemen who move around a place to guard it

patter   to make the light, tapping sound rain makes against a window

pattern   **1** a set of lines and shapes drawn on something to make it look pretty
2 anything that people copy in order to make something
a dress pattern

pause   to stop for a very short time

pavement   the part at each side of a street for people to walk along safely

pavilion   the building where people playing games such as cricket can leave their things or wait for their turn

paw   an animal's foot

pay   to give money in return for something
I paid for the sweets last time.

pea   a tiny, round, green vegetable that grows inside a pod

peace   **1** a time free from war
2 a time of quiet and rest
We enjoy the peace and quiet when the baby is asleep.

peaceful   quiet

peach   a round, soft, juicy fruit with a large stone and a thin, yellow skin

peacock   a large bird with very long, brightly coloured tail feathers that it can spread out like a fan

peak   **1** the top of a mountain
2 the part of a cap that sticks out in front

peal   to make a loud, ringing sound

peanut   a tiny, round nut that grows in a pod in the ground

pear   a juicy fruit that is narrow where the stalk is

pearl   a small, shiny, white ball found inside the shells of some oysters. Pearls are used for making valuable jewellery.

a pearl necklace

peat soil that is formed from decaying plants. It can be dug up in solid pieces and burnt instead of coal.

pebble a small, round stone

peck to use the beak to pick up food or push at something

peculiar strange
a peculiar taste

pedal a part that is pressed with the foot to make something work. A bicycle has two pedals.

pedestrian someone who is walking

peel the skin on some fruit and vegetables

peep to look quickly or secretly

peer to get very close to something to look at it
They peered at the writing and tried to read it.

pelican a sea bird with a very large beak

pelicans

pellet a tiny ball of wet paper, metal, food, or medicine

pelt 1 an animal's hair and skin
2 to throw a lot of things at someone
They pelted the boys with snowballs.

penalty a kind of punishment
The referee gave a penalty against us to the other side.

pence more than one **penny**

pencil a thin wooden stick with another coloured stick inside it, used for writing and drawing

pendant something hung round the neck on a long chain or string

pendulum a rod with a weight hanging from its end so that it swings backwards and forwards. Some clocks are worked by pendulums.

penetrate to make or find a way through something
The cold wind penetrated even his winter coat.

penguin a sea bird that cannot fly and uses its short, stiff wings for swimming

penguins

penknife a small knife that folds up so that you can carry it with you safely

penny a coin
100 pence = £1
She counted out six pennies.

people men, women, and children

pepper   a powder used to give food a stronger flavour. It can make you sneeze.

peppermint   a sweet with a strong mint flavour

perch   **1** anything that a bird rests on when it is not flying
2 to sit on the edge of something, like a bird on a branch

percussion instrument   any musical instrument that is banged, hit, or shaken. Drums, cymbals, and tambourines are percussion instruments

perfect   so good that it cannot be made any better

perform   to do something in front of an audience

performance   something done in front of an audience
The last performance of the play was on Friday night.

perfume   a liquid with a very sweet smell

perhaps   possibly
Perhaps it will rain tomorrow.

peril   danger
the perils of the sea

perimeter   the distance round the edge of something

perish   **1** to die
The sailors perished in the storm.
2 to become dry and wrinkled and no longer any use. Rubber perishes.

permanent   able to last for a very long time without changing
This ink is permanent – it won't wash out.

permission   words that say something is allowed
They got permission to go to the cinema.

permit   to allow
Weather permitting, we shall go for a walk this afternoon.

persist   to carry on doing something no matter what happens
The child persisted in crying for more, even though the sweet packet was empty.

person   a man, woman, or child

persuade   to get someone to agree to something
She persuaded her mum to buy her the coat.

pest   any person, animal, or plant that causes a lot of trouble
Flies are a pest.

pester   to keep worrying someone by asking questions
He pestered his dad about getting a new bike.

petal   one of the separate, coloured parts of a flower. Daisies have a lot of white petals.

petrol   a liquid made from oil. Petrol is put in the engines of things such as cars and aeroplanes to make them go.

petticoat   a piece of clothing worn underneath dresses and skirts

pew   one of the long wooden seats in a church

phone   short for **telephone**

photo, photograph   a picture taken with a camera and printed on paper

phrase   a group of words, such as *at the seaside*

physical   having to do with the body *physical education*

piano   a large musical instrument with white and black keys that are pressed with the fingers

pick   **1** to choose
2 to take something up from where it is
Pick up that sweet paper.
3 to take flowers or fruit from plants and trees
4 a pickaxe

pickaxe   a heavy tool with a long handle, for breaking up very hard ground

pickles   vegetables stored in vinegar

picnic   a meal eaten in the open air away from home

picture   a painting, drawing, or photograph

pie   meat or fruit covered with pastry and baked

piece   a part of something
a piece of cake

pier   something long that is built out into the sea for people to walk on. Some piers have shops on them and places where people can enjoy themselves.

pierce   to make a hole through something
The straw pierced the bottle top.

pigeon   a bird that can be taught to fly home from far away

pile   a number of things put on top of one another

pilgrim   someone who makes a journey to a holy place

pill   a small, round tablet

pillar   a wooden or stone post that helps to hold up a building

pillion   the seat on a motorbike behind the rider's seat

pillow   the cushion that you rest your head on in bed

pilot   **1** someone who steers an aeroplane
2 someone who steers a ship in narrow, difficult places

pimple   a small, round swelling on the skin

pincers   a tool for holding something tightly

pinch   **1** to squeeze skin between the thumb and finger in order to hurt someone
2 to take without asking
Who's pinched my pencil?

pine   **1** to get ill because you miss someone very much
The dog pined for his master who was on holiday.
2 a tree with cones for its seeds and clusters of leaves that look like green needles

pineapple   a large fruit that grows in hot countries. It has stiff, pointed leaves and a thick skin covered in lumps.

pint   a measure for liquid
a pint of milk

pioneer   **1** one of the first people to go and live in a new country
2 someone who is the first to do something

pipe   **1** a tube for taking gas or water somewhere
2 a tube with a small bowl at one end, used for smoking tobacco

pirate   someone on a ship, who attacks and robs other ships

pistol   a small gun

pitch   **1** ground marked out for cricket, football, or another game
2 a black, sticky liquid made from tar
3 to put up a tent
4 to throw
He pitched the ball high over our heads.

pitchfork   a tool like a very large fork, for lifting hay

pity   the feeling you have when you are sorry that someone is in pain or trouble

pivot   a point that things swing from, spin round, or balance on. Wheels and see-saws have pivots.

pivot

pixie, pixy   a kind of fairy
Do you believe in pixies and goblins?

pizza
a flat piece of dough covered with tomatoes, cheese, and other things, and then baked

placard   a notice

place   **1** any space where something belongs
2 to put something in a particular place

plague   a dangerous illness that spreads very quickly

plaice   a sea fish that can be eaten
(See picture on p. 220)

plain   **1** not decorated
a plain sponge cake
2 not pretty
3 easy to understand
The meaning is plain.
4 a large area of flat ground
On the plain you could see for miles around.

plait   (*say* plat)
1 to twist together pieces of wool, cord, thread, straw, or hair by crossing them over and under each other
2 a long piece of plaited hair

plan　**1** to decide what is going to be done
2 a map of a building or town

plane　**1** short for **aeroplane**
2 a tool for making wood smooth
3 a tall tree with large leaves

planet　any of the worlds in space that move round the sun. The earth is a planet. (See p. 224)

plank　a long, flat piece of wood

plant　anything that grows out of the ground. Trees, bushes, and flowers are all plants.

plaster　**1** a sticky strip of special material for covering cuts
2 a soft mixture that goes hard when it dries. Plaster is used in building, mending broken bones, and making models.

plastic　something light and strong that is made in factories and used for making all kinds of things
plastic bowls, plastic bags

plasticine　something like clay only soft and coloured, which you can make into different shapes with your hands

plate　a flat dish for eating from

platform　**1** a small stage
The teacher stood on the platform to speak to the whole school.
2 the place in a station where people wait beside the railway lines for a train

play　**1** to be in a game
2 to make music with a musical instrument
3 a story that is acted
He went to the theatre to see a play.

playground　a place out of doors where children can play

playing-card　one of a set of cards used in some games

playtime　the time at school when children can go out to play

plead　to beg for something that you want very much
She pleaded with her parents to buy a dog.

pleasant　pleasing
a pleasant holiday

please　**1** to make someone happy
2 the polite word you use when you are asking for something
Please may I have another cake?

pleasure　the feeling people have when they are pleased

pleat　**1** a flat fold made in the material of a dress, skirt, or kilt
2 *pleated* with pleats

plenty　**1** a lot of something
There was plenty of food for everyone.
2 more than enough
No more crisps, you've had plenty.

pliers　a tool for holding something tightly or for bending or breaking wire

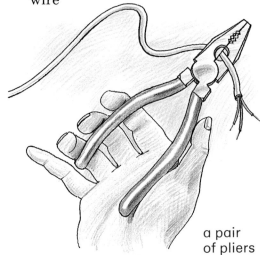

a pair
of pliers

plimsoll　a light, canvas shoe with a rubber sole

plod　to walk slowly and heavily

plot 1 to plan secretly
They plotted how to trick him.
2 a small piece of ground
They cleared a plot to grow vegetables.

plough (*rhymes with* cow)
a machine used on farms for digging and turning over the soil

plough

pluck 1 to pull a feather, flower, or fruit from the place where it is growing
2 to pull at something and let it go quickly. People play guitars by plucking the strings.

plucky brave
The plucky boy dived in to save the drowning cat.

plug 1 a part joined to a lamp or machine by wire. It fits into a place in a wall where electricity can come into it. (See picture on p. 222)
2 a round piece of rubber or metal that fits into a hole. It stops water running out of a bath or sink.

plum a juicy fruit with a stone in it

plumber someone who puts in and mends taps and water pipes

plume a large feather

plump fat

plunge 1 to jump suddenly into water
2 to put something suddenly into water
He plunged the burning cloth into a bowl of water.

plural any word when it is written differently to show that it means more than one. *Cakes, children, ladies, mice,* and *monkeys* are all plurals.

plus add. Three plus three is six, 3 + 3 = 6.

plywood a kind of wood made from thin sheets of wood glued together

pneumonia (*say* new-monia)
a serious illness that makes it painful to breathe

poach 1 to cook an egg in boiling water or steam without its shell
2 to hunt animals that are on someone else's land

pocket a part like a small bag, sewn into some clothes

pod a long seed case that grows on some plants. Peas grow inside pods.

poem a piece of writing with a special rhythm. Poems are usually written out in short lines.

poet someone who writes poetry

poetry poems

point 1 the sharp end of things such as pins and pencils
2 a mark scored in a game
3 to show where something is by holding out your finger towards it
4 to aim a weapon

pointed with a point at the end

poison any liquid, powder, or plant that will kill or harm you if you swallow it

poisonous   likely to harm you because it contains poison
poisonous berries

poke   to push hard with the end of your finger or a stick

poker   a metal rod for poking a fire

polar bear   a very large, white bear that lives in the Arctic

pole   **1** a long, round stick of wood or metal
2 either of the two ends of a magnet
3 *North pole* the place that is the furthest north in the world
4 *South pole* the place that is the furthest south in the world

police   the people whose job is to catch criminals and make sure that the law is kept. There are thousands of **policemen** and **policewomen** in Britain.

polish   to rub the surface of something to make it shine

polite   having good manners

pollen   the yellow powder inside a flower. Pollen helps to make seeds.

pollution   dirty and unhealthy air or water. Smoke and waste from factories cause pollution.

pond   a very small lake

ponder   to think about something carefully

pony   a small horse

poodle   a kind of dog with curly hair often cut very short on some parts of its body (See picture on p. 220)

pool   **1** a small area of water
2 a game like snooker

poor   **1** having very little money
a poor family
2 bad
poor work, poor light

poplar   a tall, straight tree
(See picture on p. 219)

poppy   a bright red flower often found growing near corn

poppies

popular   liked by a lot of people

population   the number of people who live in a place

porch   a small place with a roof, in front of the door of a building

pork   meat from a pig

porpoise   a sea animal like a small whale

porridge   a hot food made from oats boiled in water or milk, eaten at breakfast

port   a large place where ships can stay safely in the water when they are not at sea

portable   able to be carried about
a portable television

porter   someone whose job is to carry other people's luggage at places like hotels and railway stations

portion   the part or amount given to you
Get a small portion of chips.

portrait   a picture of a person

posh   very smart

position   1 the place where something is or should be
This is a good position to pitch the tent.
2 how the body and its parts are arranged
a sitting position

positive   completely sure
I am positive I gave you the book.

possess   to own
She possessed five pairs of shoes.

possible   able to happen or to be done
It is possible it might snow tonight.

post   1 an upright pole fixed in the ground
2 to send a letter, parcel, or card

postcard   a piece of card that you can write a message on and post. Postcards often have pictures on one side.

postcode   a group of letters and numbers that show the district a person lives in, so that the post office can deliver the mail more quickly

poster   a large notice for everyone to read

postman   someone who collects and delivers letters and parcels

post office   a place that sells stamps and deals with letters and parcels

postpone   to put off until later
They postponed the race until the rain had stopped.

potato   a vegetable dug out of the ground
baked potatoes

potion   a drink with medicine or poison in it

pottery   cups, plates, and other things made out of baked clay

pouch   1 a small bag
2 a kind of pocket that some animals have in their skin. Hamsters have pouches inside their cheeks.

pouffe   (*rhymes with* roof)
a low seat that is like a large, firm cushion

poultry   birds kept for their meat and eggs
Hens and turkeys are poultry.

pounce   to attack something by jumping on it suddenly
The rat pounced on the mouse.

pound   **1** a measure for weight
five pounds of potatoes
2 a measure for money, also written £
£1 = 100 pence
3 to beat very hard with the fists
He pounded on the door to make them hear.
4 to crush something by hitting it very hard

pour   **1** to make liquid run out of a container
2 *to pour with rain* to rain hard

pout   to stick out your lips when you are not pleased

powder   anything that is very dry and made up of many separate tiny bits, like flour or dust

power   **1** the ability to do something
2 strength

powerful   very strong or important

practical   **1** able to do useful things
A penknife is a practical gadget.
2 likely to be useful
a practical idea

practice   something you keep doing in order to get better at it
piano practice

practise   to do something over and over again in order to get better at doing it
If you keep practising you will soon improve.

prairie   a very large area of flat ground covered in grass. in North America

praise   to say that someone or something is very good

pram   a kind of cot on wheels for a baby

prance   to jump about in a very lively way
a prancing horse

pray   to talk to God

prayer   talking to God

preach   to speak to other people just as a priest does in church

precious   very valuable
a precious jewel

precipice   a very steep part of a mountain or rock

prefer   to like one person or thing more than another person or thing
She preferred singing to dancing.

pregnant   expecting a baby

prehistoric   belonging to a time very long ago
prehistoric animals

preparations   things that are done to get ready for something
The preparations for Christmas start in October.

prepare   to get something ready

present[1] (*say* <u>prez</u>-ent)
  1 something given to someone
  a birthday present
  2 the time now
  Our teacher is away at present.
  3 here
  All present and correct, sir!

present[2] (*say* pri-<u>zent</u>)
  to give someone a prize or gift in front of other people

presently soon

preserve **1** to keep safe
  2 to do things to food so that it will not go bad

president someone chosen to rule a country that does not have a king or queen

press **1** to push hard on something
  Press the doorbell.
  2 to make clothes smooth and flat with an iron

pressure **1** pressing on something
  The pressure of the pile of books squashed the box.
  2 how much one thing is pressing on another
  Test the air pressure of the car tyre.

pretend to make it seem that something not true is true
  He pretended he was ill.

pretty pleasant to look at
  a pretty girl, a pretty dress

prevent to stop something from happening
  You can prevent pollution.

previous coming before this one
  the previous week

prey **1** any animal hunted and eaten by another animal
  2 *a bird of prey* a bird that hunts and eats other animals

price the amount of money you have to pay for something

priceless very valuable

prick to make a tiny hole in something

prickle a sharp part like a thorn

pride the feeling people have when they are proud

priest **1** someone who serves God by being in charge of a church
  2 a man who leads people in their religion

primary school the school you go to from when you are about five years old until you are about twelve

Prime Minister the most important person in the government

primrose a small, pale yellow flower that comes out early in the spring

primroses

prince the son of a king or queen

princess **1** the daughter of a king or queen
  2 the wife of a prince

principal most important or chief

principle an important rule

print **1** to write with letters that are not joined together
  2 to use a machine that presses words and pictures on to paper. Books, newspapers, and magazines are printed.

prison a place where criminals are kept as a punishment

prisoner **1** someone who has been captured
2 someone in prison

private **1** not open to everyone
a private road
2 not known by other people
a private thought

prize something that is won

probable likely to be true or to happen
What's the most probable result?

problem something that is difficult to understand or to answer

proceed to go on
The carnival parade proceeded slowly along the street.

procession a group of people moving along in a long line

prod to push something with the end of a finger or stick

produce **1** to make
2 to bring something out so that it can be seen

producer the person in charge of the acting of a play

profit the extra money got by selling something for more than it cost to buy or make

program a list of instructions for a computer

```
1Ø  CLS
2Ø  LET X = 1Ø: Let Y = 1Ø
3Ø  Let A$ = INKEY$
4Ø  IF A$ = "" THEN GOTO 3Ø
5Ø  IF A$ = "A" THEN LET Y = Y-1
6Ø  IF A$ = "Z" THEN LET Y = Y+1
7Ø  IF A$ = "N" THEN LET X = X-1
```

programme **1** a talk, play, or show on the radio or television
2 a list for people in an audience telling them about what they will see or hear

progress **1** moving forward
We've been in the queue for an hour but we're making slow progress.
2 getting better
All the class made good progress in arithmetic.

prohibit to say that people must not do something
Smoking Prohibited

project **1** finding out as much as you can about something interesting and writing about it
a project on flight
2 a plan

projector a machine for showing films or photographs on a screen

promenade a kind of road near the sea where people can walk

promise to say that you will certainly do or not do something
He's always promising us things.

prompt without delay

prong one of the thin, pointed parts on the end of a fork

pronounce to say a sound or word in a certain way

proof something that shows that an idea is true

prop **1** a long piece of wood or metal put underneath something to support it
2 to support one thing by leaning it against another thing
The ladder was propped up against the wall.

propel to drive forward

propeller   a set of blades that spin round. Propellers are fixed to aeroplanes, helicopters, and ships to make them move. (See picture on p. 215)

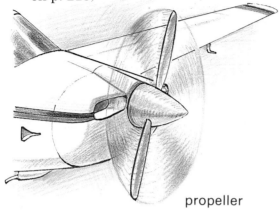

propeller

proper   correct
in the proper place

property   things that belong to someone

prophet   someone who tells people what is going to happen, although nobody knows

prosecute   to make someone go to court so that they can be punished if they have done wrong
Trespassers will be prosecuted

prosper   to become successful or rich

protect   to keep safe from danger

protection   something that protects

protest   to say or show that you think what someone else is saying or doing is wrong

proud   1 full of the idea that you are better or more important than you really are
2 very pleased because you, or someone belonging to you, has done well
He is proud of his sister.

prove   to show that an idea is true

proverb   something often said in order to help people, such as 'A stitch in time saves nine,' or, 'Too many cooks spoil the broth.'

provide   to give something that is needed

prowl   to move about like an animal looking for something to kill and eat

prune   a dried plum

pry   to try to find out about something that has nothing to do with you
He liked to pry into other people's business.

psalm   (*say* sarm)
one of the hymns in the Bible

public   1 all the people
the general public
2 open to everyone
Everyone came to the public meeting.

pudding   something sweet and made to be eaten after the main part of a meal

a Christmas pudding

puddle   a small pool of dirty water

puff   1 a small amount of breath, wind, or smoke
2 to blow out puffs of smoke or air
3 *puffed* out of breath

puffin   a sea bird with a large orange and blue beak

pull   to get hold of something and make it come towards you

pulley   a wheel with rope round it, used for lifting heavy things
They lifted the car engine using a pulley.

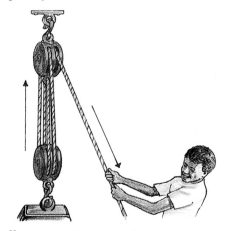

pullover   a jersey or jumper

pulp   anything that has been made soft and wet
fruit pulp, paper pulp

pulpit   the high wooden desk in a church, where the priest stands to talk to the people

pulse   the throbbing that can be felt at the wrist as the blood is pumped around inside the body

pump   1 a machine that pushes liquid or air through pipes
She filled the car with petrol from the pump.
2 to push air or liquid into something
Pump up that flat tyre.

pumpkin   a very large, round fruit with a hard yellow skin

punch   1 to hit with the fist
2 a tool for making holes in paper or leather

punctual   exactly on time
Please be punctual or the coach will leave without you.

punctuation   marks such as commas and full stops put into a piece of writing to make it easier to read

puncture   a hole in a tyre

punish   to make someone who has done wrong suffer, so that they will not want to do wrong again
People who break the law are punished and sent to prison.

punishment   something done to punish someone

pupil   1 someone who has a teacher
2 the black spot at the centre of the eye

puppet   1 a kind of doll whose head and limbs can be moved by strings and rods
2 a kind of doll with a body like a glove, so that you can move its head and arms with your fingers

puppet 2

puppet 1

138

puppy   a very young dog

purchase   to buy

pure   with nothing else mixed with it
pure water

purpose   what someone means to do
He trod on my toe on purpose not by accident.

purr   to make the sound a cat makes when it is very pleased

purse   a small bag for holding money

pursue   to run after someone and try to catch them
The policeman pursued the thief.

push   to use your hands to move something away from you

put   to move something into a place

putty   something soft and sticky that sets hard, used for fixing glass into windows

puzzle   **1** a game or question that is difficult to work out and makes you think a lot
a crossword puzzle
2 to make someone think very hard to find the answer
a puzzling question

pyjamas   trousers and a jacket worn in bed

pylon   a metal tower that holds up high electric cables

pyramid   **1** a large, stone building made by the ancient Egyptians to hold the body of a dead king or queen. Pyramids have sloping sides that meet in a point at the top.
2 the shape of a pyramid
(See the list of shapes on p. 223)

python   a very large snake

Q q

quack   to make the sound a duck makes

quadrilateral   a flat shape with four sides and four corners

quail   **1** a wild bird that can be eaten
2 to look frightened

quaint   unusual but pleasant
a quaint cottage

quake   to shake because you are very frightened
She was quaking with fear.

quality   how good or bad something is
You need best quality paper for model-making.

quantity   an amount
She added a small quantity of salt to the dough.

quarrel   to speak angrily to someone or fight with them, because they do not agree with you
He often quarrelled with his brother.

quarry   **1** a place where people cut stone out of the ground so that it can be used for building
2 an animal that is being hunted
In a fox-hunt the fox is the quarry.

quarter   one of the four equal parts something can be divided into. It can also be written as ¼.

quay   (*say* key)
a place where ships can be loaded and unloaded

queen   **1** a woman who has been crowned as ruler of a country
2 a king's wife

queer   very strange
a queer feeling

quench **1** to put an end to someone's thirst
The tea quenched her thirst.
2 to use water to put out a fire
The bucket of water quenched the spreading flames.

query (*say* queery)
a question that you ask about something, because you think it might be wrong
She had a query about the plans.

quest a long search
The knight set off on a quest to find lost treasure.

question something that you ask when you want to find out or get something

queue (*say* cue)
a line of people waiting for something

quick **1** done in less time than usual
a quick snack
2 fast
Be quick!

quiet **1** without any noise
2 not loud
a quiet voice

quill **1** a big feather from a bird's wing or tail
2 a pen made from a feather

quilt a bed cover like an eiderdown. It has lines of stitching across it to keep the filling in place.

quite **1** completely
I'm quite sure.
2 *quite big* big, but not enormous

quiver **1** to shake because you are very cold or frightened
2 a bag for carrying arrows

quiz a kind of game in which people try to answer a lot of questions in order to show how much they know
Do you like quizzes?

R r

rabbi a teacher of Judaism

rabbit a furry animal with long ears. Rabbits live in holes they have dug in the ground.

race a competition to find the fastest

rack a set of bars made into a shelf or something else that people can put things on
a luggage rack

racket **1** a kind of bat with a wooden or metal frame and string stretched across it in a criss-cross pattern
a tennis racket
2 a lot of loud noise
What a racket all those barking dogs made.

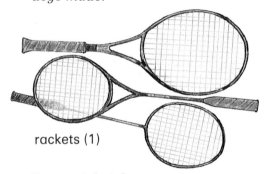

rackets (1)

radiant **1** bright
radiant sunshine
2 looking very happy
a radiant smile

radiate to give out heat or light
Warmth radiated from the fire.

radiator **1** a metal container or a set of pipes that gives out heat in a room
2 the part inside a car for keeping the engine cool

radio a machine that receives sounds sent as electrical waves and changes them into words and music that people can listen to

radish a small, hard, round, red vegetable, eaten raw in salads

radius the distance from the centre of a circle to the edge
two radii

raffle a kind of sale held to get money for something. People buy tickets with numbers on them and certain numbers win prizes.

raft something flat made of pieces of wood joined together and used instead of a boat (See picture on p. 215)

rafter one of the long, sloping pieces of wood that hold up a roof

rage great anger

raid a sudden attack on a place

rail 1 a bar or rod
2 a long metal bar that is part of a railway line

railings a fence made of metal bars

railway the set of metal bars that trains travel on

rain drops of water that fall from the sky

rainbow the curved band of different colours seen in the sky when the sun shines through rain

raincoat a coat made of waterproof material for keeping you dry when it rains

raise 1 to lift up or make something higher
2 to gather together the money or people needed for something
We need to raise money for the school trip.

raisin a dried grape used in cooking

rake a tool used in the garden. It has a long handle and a row of short spikes at one end.

rally a large number of people who have come together for a big meeting

ram 1 a male sheep
2 to push one thing very hard into another thing
She rammed the cork into the bottle.

Ramadan a holy time for Muslims when they fast during the day

ramble a long walk in the country

ran see **run**

ranch a large American farm with a lot of cattle or horses

random *at random* without any plan or aim

rang see **ring**

rank 1 a title or job that shows how important someone is. The rank of general is higher than the rank of captain.
2 a row of people
The soldiers stood in neat ranks.

ransack to search everywhere for something and leave things looking very untidy

ransom money paid so that a prisoner can be set free

rap to knock quickly and loudly
She rapped on the door and told them to hurry up.

rapid very quick

rare not often found. Pandas are rare animals.

rascal 1 a naughty child
2 someone who is not honest

rash 1 done in a rush without any thought about what might happen
a rash action
2 red spots or patches that suddenly come on the skin
a measles rash

raspberry a soft, sweet, red berry

raspberries

rate how quickly something happens or is done

rather 1 fairly
It's rather cold.
2 more willingly
I'd rather have a cake.

rattle 1 to make quick, hard noises by shaking something
2 a baby's toy that rattles

rave to talk in a very excited or enthusiastic way
He raved about his holiday saying it was his best ever.

raven a large, black bird

ravenous very hungry
She had missed her breakfast and lunch and was ravenous at supper.

ravine (*say* ra-v<u>een</u>)
a very deep, narrow space between mountains

raw not cooked

ray a thin line of light
the sun's rays

razor a very thin, sharp blade. Men shave their faces with razors.

reach 1 to stretch out the hand in order to touch something
He reached for a cake.
2 to arrive at a place

reaction an action in reply to something that has happened or has been done
What was Dad's reaction to the broken window?

read[1] (*say* reed)
to be able to say and understand words that are written down
I've read this before.

read[2] (*say* red)
see **read**[1]

ready 1 able and willing to do something at once
Are you ready yet?
2 fit to be used at once
Everything is ready.

real   not a copy
a real diamond

realize   to come to understand something clearly
He realized that the furry lump was in fact a kitten.

really   truly
Is it really snowing?

realm   (*rhymes with* helm)
the land a king or queen rules

reap   to cut down and gather in the corn when it is ready

rear   **1** the back part of something
Sit at the rear of the bus.
2 to look after children or young animals until they are big
She reared the puppies.
3 to stand on the back legs and lift the front legs into the air, like a dog begging
The horse reared in fright when it saw the snake.

reason   anything that explains why something has happened

reasonable   **1** fair
a reasonable price
2 sensible
It is not reasonable to play outside in the rain.

rebel¹   (*say* ri-<u>bell</u>)
to decide not to obey the people in charge
The soldiers rebelled.

rebel²   (*say* <u>reb</u>-el)
someone who rebels

recall   to remember
The old man could clearly recall his school-days.

receive   to get something that has been given or sent to you
Did you receive a letter this morning?

recent   made or done a short time ago
A recent record by this group was very popular.

recipe   (*say* re-si-pee)
instructions that tell you how to cook something

recite   to say a poem or something else that you have learnt by heart

reckless   likely to do silly or dangerous things. Reckless people do things without thinking or caring about what might happen.

reckon   **1** to count or add up
She quickly reckoned the cost of repairing the window.
2 to think something and feel sure it is right
I reckon that with all our skill our team should win.

recognize   to know who someone is because you have seen them before

record   **1** a flat, round piece of black plastic that makes music or other sounds while it is turning round on a record-player
2 the best that has been done so far in a sport or hobby
He broke the world record in that race.
3 to put music or other sounds on a tape or disc

recorder   a wooden or plastic musical instrument shaped like a tube, that you blow

record-player a machine that makes sounds come out of records

recover **1** to get better after being ill
2 to get something back that you have lost
He recovered the bag that he had left on the bus.

recreation hobbies or games people like playing in their spare time

rectangle the shape of a postcard
(See the list of shapes on p. 223)

reduce to make smaller or less
She reduced speed as she got near the roundabout.

reed a large grass with a strong stem that grows near water

reef a line of rocks just below or just above the surface of the sea

reek to have a strong smell that is not pleasant
The room reeked of stale cigarette smoke.

reel **1** a round piece of wood or metal that cotton, string, fishing line, or film is wound round
Put a new reel of film in the camera.
2 a Scottish dance
3 to lose your balance because you feel dizzy

reel

refer **1** to say a little about something while talking about other things
2 to look in a book for information or facts

referee someone who makes sure that the players in a game keep to the rules

reference book a book that gives you information. Dictionaries are reference books.

reflect **1** to send back light from a shiny surface. Water often reflects the light of the sun.
2 to show a picture of something, as a mirror does
The trees were reflected in the clear water.

reflection a picture seen in a mirror or water

refresh to make a tired person feel fresh and strong again
a refreshing drink

refreshments drinks and snacks

refrigerator a kind of metal cupboard that keeps food and drink cold and fresh, often called a **fridge**

refuse[1] (*say* ri-<u>fuse</u>)
1 to say you will not do something you have been asked to do
She refused to tidy her room.
2 to say you do not want what someone is offering you
He refused a third cream-cake.

refuse[2] (*say* <u>ref</u>-yoos)
rubbish

regard to think of someone or something in a certain way
He regarded the football player as his hero.

regiment a large, organized group of soldiers

region a part of a country or the world
Snow covers the northern regions of the earth all year round.

register an important book with a list of names and addresses in it
a school register

regret the feeling you have when you are sorry about something
She regretted she had been cross when she saw he was upset.

regular **1** usual **2** always happening at certain times
regular meals

rehearsal a practice for a concert or play

rehearse to practise something before it is done in front of an audience

reign **1** to be king or queen
You will reign over the land for the rest of your life.
2 the time when someone is king or queen
Many changes took place during her reign.

reindeer a kind of deer that lives in very cold countries

reins the two long straps used for guiding a horse

rejoice to be very happy about something
The school rejoiced at their team's success.

relation a relative

relative someone in the same family as you

relax to rest the body by letting it become less stiff
She relaxed in the warm bath.

relay race a race between teams in which each person does part of the distance

release to set someone free

relent to be less angry than you were going to be
She relented and let them watch the programme.

reliable able to be trusted
a reliable person

relic something very old that was left by people who lived long ago

relief the feeling you have when you are no longer in trouble, pain, or danger

relieved happy because you are no longer in trouble, pain, or danger
They were relieved to see the helicopter coming to rescue them.

religion   what people believe about God and the way they worship

reluctant   not willing to do something
He was reluctant to set off as it was raining.

rely   to trust someone or something to help you
The blind man relied on his dog.

remain   **1** to stay
The sign remained long after the circus had gone.
2 to be left behind
Very little food remained after their picnic.

remainder   what is left over
Ten children went swimming. The remainder played tennis.

remark   to say something that you have thought or noticed

remarkable   so unusual that you remember it

remedy   something that cures an illness
An old remedy for curing warts is supposed to be counting them.

remember   to be able to bring something into your mind when you want to

remind   to make or help someone remember something

remote   far away
Does your T.V. have remote control?

a remote control

removal van   a van for moving the things inside a house to a different house

remove   to take something away

rent   an amount of money paid every week or month for the use of something that belongs to another person

repair   to mend
She repaired the hole in the roof.

repeat   to say or do the same thing again

repent   to be very sorry about something you have said or done
She repented, after being unkind.

replace   **1** to put something back
He replaced the book on the shelf.
2 to take the place of another person or thing
We have a new car to replace the old one.

reply   to answer
You must reply to her letter.

report   to tell or write news

represent   **1** to speak or do things in place of another person or a group of people
The girls represented the school in the competition.
2 to be a picture or model of something
This picture represents our school in the last century.

reptile   an animal with cold blood that creeps or crawls. Snakes, crocodiles, and tortoises are all reptiles.

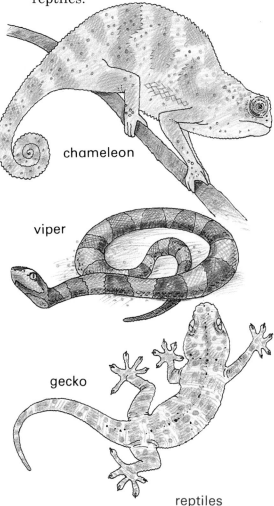

chameleon

viper

gecko

reptiles

reputation   the things everyone says or thinks about a person

request   to ask politely for something

require   to need

rescue   to save from danger

resemble   to look or sound like another person or thing
He resembled his father.

reserve   **1** to keep for later
She reserved some seeds to plant next year.
2 someone ready to take part in a game if a member of the team cannot play
The reserve waited at the side of the pitch.

reservoir   a place where a very large amount of water is stored

resist   to fight against something and not give way
He resisted all their attempts to make him change his mind.

resolve   to decide
She resolved to try harder at dancing.

respect   the feeling you have for someone you like and admire

responsible   in charge and likely to take the blame if anything goes wrong

rest   **1** to lie down, lean against something, or sit without doing anything
2 the part that is left
Eat as much as you can: the dog can have the rest.
3 the other people or things
You stay, but the rest can go.

restaurant   a place where you can buy a meal and eat it

restore   to make something as good as it was before
The ruined church was restored.

result   **1** anything that happens because of other things that have happened
2 the score or marks at the end of a game, competition, or test

retire   to stop working because you are too old or ill
My grandmother is retiring soon.

retreat   to go back because it is too dangerous to carry on

return   **1** to come back to a place **2** to give something back

reveal   to let something be seen or known
He moved the paper and revealed the presents.

revenge   a wish to hurt someone because they have hurt you or one of your friends

reverse   **1** the opposite side or way **2** to go backwards in a car

revolt   **1** to say that you will not obey the people in charge
2 *revolting* so nasty that you feel sick

revolution   a great struggle to get rid of the government by force and put a new kind of government in its place

revolver   a small gun that can be fired several times without having to be loaded again

reward   a present given to someone because of something they have done

rhinoceros   a very large, heavy animal found in Africa and Asia. Rhinoceroses have horns on their noses.

rhubarb   a plant with pink stalks that are cooked and eaten with sugar

rhyme   (*say* rime)
A word that has the same sound at the end as another word. *Bat* and *mat* are rhymes and so are *batter* and *matter*.

rhythm   (*say* ri-them)
the pattern made in music or poetry by the strong and weak sounds

rib   one of the curved bones above the waist

ribbon   a strip of nylon, silk, or some other material

rice   shiny white seeds that are cooked in liquid. The seeds come from a kind of grass grown in marshes in hot countries.

rice plants

rich   having a lot of money

rick   a neat pile of straw or hay

ridden   see **ride**

riddle   a question or puzzle that is a joke, such as
Why do Swiss cows have bells?
Because their horns don't work.

ride   **1** to sit on a horse or bicycle and control it as it moves along
Have you ridden before?
I rode her pony yesterday.
Do you like riding?
2 to travel in a car, bus, or train

ridge   a long, narrow part higher than the rest, like the line along the top of a roof

ridiculous   so silly that people might laugh at it
a ridiculous answer

rifle   a long gun that is held against the shoulder when it is fired

right   **1** on the side opposite the left. Most people hold a knife in their right hand and a fork in their left hand.
2 correct
the right answer
3 fair
It is not right to cheat.
4 completely
Turn it right round.

right-handed   using the right hand to write and do other important things, because you find it easier than using the left hand

rim   the edge round the top of a round container or round the outside of a wheel

rind   the skin on bacon, cheese, or fruit

ring   **1** a circle
2 a circle of thin metal worn on the finger
3 to make a bell sound
I've rung your bell twice.
4 to telephone
He rang up the police an hour ago.

ring-master   the person with a top hat and a whip who is in charge of what happens in the circus ring

rink   an area of ice or ground for skating on

rinse   to wash something in clean water

riot   a large group of people shouting and fighting

rip   to tear

ripe   ready to be gathered or eaten
ripe fruit

ripen   to become ripe
The fruit will ripen in the sun.

ripple   a tiny movement on the surface of water

rise   **1** to go upwards
The sun has already risen.
Prices are rising.
2 to get up
They all rose as she came in.

risk   the chance of danger

rival   someone trying to win the same prize as you are

river   a large stream

road   a way with a hard surface made for people, animals, and traffic to go along

roam   to move around without trying to get anywhere
They roamed all over the hills.

roar   to make the loud, deep sound a lion makes

roast   to cook meat or vegetables inside the oven with fat

robber   someone who steals and is ready to hurt people who get in their way

robbery   taking things by force from other people
a bank robbery

robin   a small, brown bird with a red patch on its front.

robot   a machine that can move and behave like a person

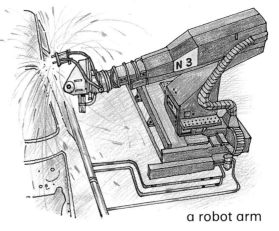

a robot arm

rock **1** something very hard and heavy that is part of the mountains, the hills, and the ground
2 a hard sweet shaped like a stick and sold at the seaside
3 to move gently backwards and forwards or from side to side

rocket **1** a firework joined to a stick. Rockets shoot high into the air when they are lit.
2 a tall metal tube that is used to launch spacecraft. Hot gases rush out of it at the bottom and the spacecraft takes off.

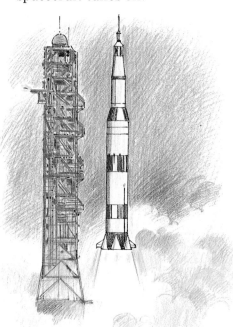

rocket 2

rod a long, thin, round piece of wood or metal

rode see **ride**

rogue someone who is not honest

roll **1** a cylinder made by rolling something up
2 a very small loaf of bread
3 to turn over and over like a ball moving along the ground

roller **1** a heavy cylinder rolled over things to make them flat or smooth
a road roller
2 a small cylinder put in hair to curl it
a hair roller

roller-boot a set of small wheels that are fitted into a boot and make you able to move quickly and smoothly over the ground

roller-boots

rolling-pin a wooden cylinder rolled over pastry to make it flat

roof the part that covers the top of a building

room **1** one of the spaces with walls round it inside a building. Bathrooms, kitchens, and lounges are rooms.
2 enough space for something

roost the place where a bird rests at night

root the part of a plant that grows under the ground

rope a lot of strong threads twisted together

rose **1** a flower with a sweet smell and thorns on its stem (See picture on p. 218)
2 see **rise**

rosy   coloured like a pink or red rose

rot   to go soft or bad so that it cannot be used. Fruit and wood rot.

rotten   **1** very bad
a rotten player
2 so soft or bad that it cannot be used
a rotten apple, rotten wood

rough   **1** not smooth
rough wood
2 not gentle
a rough boy
3 not exact
a rough guess

round   **1** shaped like a circle or ball
2 on all sides of something
a fence round the field

roundabout   **1** a machine with seats that moves round and round. People can ride on roundabouts at fairs or in parks.
2 a place where roads meet and all traffic has to go round in the same direction

roundabout 1

rounders   a game played outside between two teams with a small ball and a bat like a heavy stick

rouse   to wake someone up

route   (*say* root)
the way you have to go to get to a place

row¹   (*rhymes with* toe)
1 people or things in a straight line
The class stood in two rows.
2 to use oars to make a boat move
He rowed the boat across the river.

row²   (*rhymes with* how)
1 a quarrel
2 a lot of noise

royal   belonging to a king or queen
the royal family

rubber   **1** a strong material that stretches, bends, and bounces. Rubber is used for making tyres, balls, elastic bands, and many other things.
2 a piece of rubber for rubbing out pencil marks

rubbish   **1** things that are not wanted or needed
2 nonsense
You're talking rubbish!

ruby   a red jewel

rudder   a flat part fixed to the end of a ship or aeroplane and used to steer it   (See picture on p. 215)

rude   not polite

rugged   (*say* rug-id)
rough and full of rocks
rugged countryside

ruin   **1** to spoil something completely
The rain ruined the corn.
2 a building that has fallen down
The castle was now a ruin.

rule   **1** something that everyone ought to obey
2 to be in charge of a country and the people who live there
3 to draw a straight line with a ruler

ruler   **1** someone who rules a country or empire
2 a strip of wood, metal, or plastic with straight edges, used for measuring and drawing straight lines

rumble   to make the deep, heavy sound thunder makes

rumour   something that a lot of people are saying, although it might not be true

run   to use the legs to move quickly
He saw the bull and ran.

rung   **1** one of the short bars on a ladder
2 see **ring**

rush   to move very quickly

rusk   a kind of biscuit for babies

rust   a rough, red surface that covers iron that has got damp or wet
The old car was covered in rust.

rustle   to make the light sounds dry leaves make when they are blown by the wind

rut   a groove made in the ground by wheels going over it many times

rye   a plant grown by farmers. Its seed is used for feeding animals and making some kinds of bread. (See picture on p. 218)

S s ——————————

sabbath   the day of the week that is set aside for rest and prayer. For some people the sabbath is Saturday but for many others it is Sunday.

sack   **1** a large bag made of strong, rough material
a sack of potatoes
2 *to get the sack* to lose your job

sacred   very holy

sacrifice   **1** to give up something you like very much in order to help someone
2 a gift offered to God

saddle   a seat put on a horse's back or on a bicycle so that you can ride it

safari   a journey made by people in order to hunt or look at lions and other wild animals

safe   **1** free from danger
2 a strong box where money or valuable things can be kept safe from thieves

safety   a time or place free from danger
The fireman carried her to safety.

sag   to go down in the middle because something heavy is pressing on it
The chair sagged under his weight.

said   see **say**

sail   **1** a large piece of strong cloth joined to a boat. The wind blows into the sail and makes the boat move (See picture on p. 215)
2 to travel in a boat

sailor   a member of a ship's crew

saint   a very holy person
St. Nicholas

sake   *for someone's sake* to help or please someone
Please do it for my sake.

salad   a mixture of vegetables eaten raw or cold

salary   money paid to someone each month for the work they do

sale   **1** the selling of things
These toys are not for sale.
2 a time when things in a shop are sold at reduced prices
The shoe shop is having a sale.

salmon   a large fish with pink flesh that you can eat (See picture on p. 220)

salt   a white powder put on food to give it flavour

salute   to touch your forehead with your hand, as soldiers do to show respect

same   not different in any way

sample   a small amount that shows what something is like

sand   the tiny bits of rock that cover deserts and ground next to the sea

sandal   a kind of light shoe with a sole and straps that go round the foot

sandwich   two slices of bread and butter with a different food between them

sang   see **sing**

sank   see **sink**

sap   the liquid inside a plant

sapling   a young tree

sardine   a small sea fish you can eat (See picture on p. 220)

sari   a kind of long dress worn by Indian women and girls

saris

sash   a strip of material tied round the waist of a dress

sat   see **sit**

satchel   a bag worn over the shoulder or on the back, for carrying books to and from school

satellite   something that moves in space around the earth or any other planet.

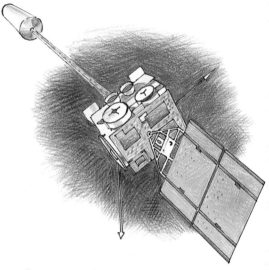

satin   smooth cloth that is very shiny on one side

satisfactory   good enough
satisfactory work

satisfy   to be good enough to please someone
Nothing satisfies him – he's always complaining.

sauce   a thick liquid put on food to make it taste better

saucepan   a metal pan with a handle and lid used for cooking things on top of a stove

saucer   a kind of small plate for putting a cup on

sausage   a skin tube stuffed with tiny pieces of meat and bread

savage   wild and fierce
a savage animal

save   **1** to free someone or something from danger
2 to keep something so that it can be used later

saw   **1** a tool with a wide, thin blade that is moved backwards and forwards across a piece of wood to cut it
2 to use a saw to cut a piece of wood
The wood was sawn in two.
I sawed it in half yesterday.
3 see **see**

saws

sawdust   a powder that comes from wood when it is cut with a saw

sawed, sawn   see **saw**

say   to use the voice to make words
He said he hadn't seen it.

saying   something wise that is often said, such as 'A stitch in time saves nine.'

scab   hard, brown skin that covers a cut or graze while it is getting better

scabbard   a cover for the blade of a sword

scaffolding   planks fixed to poles and put round a building so that workmen can stand on them while they are painting or mending it

scald   to burn yourself with very hot liquid

scales   **1** a weighing machine
a pair of scales
2 thin pieces of skin or bone that cover the outside of animals such as fish and snakes

scalp   the skin covering the top of the head where the hair grows

scamper   to run about quickly. Small dogs scamper.

scar   the mark left on the skin by a cut or burn after it has healed

scarce   **1** not enough of something
Water is scarce in deserts.
2 not often seen or found
Adders are scarce in this country.

scare   to frighten
Stop scaring me!

scarecrow   something that looks like a person and is put in a field to frighten away birds so that they will not eat the crops

scarf   a piece of material worn round the neck or head
two scarves

scarlet   bright red

scatter   to throw small things so that they fall in many different places

scene 1 the place where something happens
the scene of the crime
2 part of a play

scenery 1 painted curtains and screens put on a stage to make it look like another place
2 things such as hills, rivers, and trees that you can see around you when you are out in the country

scent 1 a liquid with a sweet smell
2 a pleasant smell
the scent of roses
3 an animal's smell
a fox's scent

scholarship money given to someone clever in order to help them to go on studying

school the place where children go to learn

science knowledge about the world that people get by studying things and testing ideas about the way they work

scientific having to do with science
a scientific experiment

scientist someone who studies science

scissors a tool for cutting that has two blades joined together
a pair of scissors

scoff to make fun of something
They scoffed at his boast that he could swim across the river.

scold to tell someone off angrily
He scolded the child for picking the flowers.

scoop 1 a deep spoon for lifting up and measuring out potato or ice cream
2 to use a tool or your arms or hands to gather things together and lift them up

scooter 1 a toy with two wheels that is ridden. You stand on it with one foot and push the other foot against the ground to make it move.
2 a kind of motorbike with a very small engine

scooter 2

scorch to make something so hot that it goes brown
The sun scorched the grass.

score 1 to get a goal or point in a game
2 the number of points or goals each side has at the end of a game
3 twenty
three score years and ten

scorn to show that you think someone or something is not worth bothering about
He scorned their offers of help.

scorpion a kind of spider with a poisonous sting in its tail

scout a soldier sent to spy on the enemy

Scout a boy who is a member of the Scout Association

scowl to make your face look unhappy and angry

scramble **1** to use your hands and feet to climb up or down something **2** *scrambled eggs* eggs mixed with milk and cooked in butter

scrap **1** a small piece
A scrap of material will make a doll's dress.
2 rubbish
That pile of wood is all scrap.

scrape to rub with something rough or sharp

scratch **1** to damage something by rubbing your nails or a sharp point over it
2 to rub your skin to stop it itching

scrawl to write with big, untidy letters

scream to make a loud cry that shows that you are very frightened or in pain

screech to make a loud, shrill sound that is not pleasant. Some owls screech.

screen **1** a smooth surface on which films or television programmes are shown
2 a kind of thin wall or a set of curtains on rails, that can be moved about. Screens are used for hiding things or protecting people.

screw **1** a kind of nail that is put into a hole and twisted in order to fasten things tightly together
2 to turn or twist something

screwdriver a tool for turning a screw until it fits tightly into something

scribble to write or draw quickly and untidily

scripture the Bible

scroll a book written on a long sheet of paper that is rolled up

scrub to rub something very hard with a brush dipped in soap and water

sculptor an artist who makes shapes and patterns in stone, wood, clay, or metal

scurry to run with fast, little steps. Mice scurry.

scuttle **1** to move quickly like a frightened mouse
2 a kind of bucket in which coal is kept

scythe (*say* sythe) a tool with a long curved blade for cutting grass

sea a very large area of salt water

sea-gull a kind of sea bird

seal **1** a furry animal that lives in the sea and on land
2 to close something by sticking two parts together
a sealed envelope

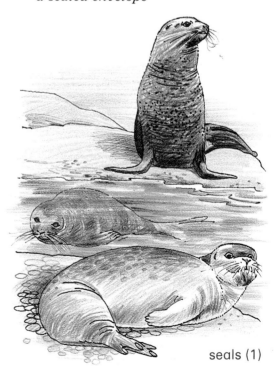

seals (1)

seam   the line where two pieces of cloth are sewn together

search   to look very carefully for something

searchlight   a strong light that can be pointed in any direction

seaside   a place by the sea where people go to enjoy themselves

season   **1** one of the four parts of the year. Spring, summer, autumn, and winter are the names of the seasons.
2 to put herbs or spices on food to make it taste better

seat   a chair or stool or anything else that people sit on

seaweed   a plant that grows in the sea

second   **1** a very small measure for time
60 seconds = 1 minute
2 coming after the first
second prize

secret   something that must be kept hidden from other people

secretary   someone whose job is to type letters, answer the telephone, and arrange things in an office

section   a part of something
This section of the book is very interesting.

secure   safe or firm
Make sure the ladder is secure before you climb it.

see   to use your eyes to get to know something
I saw an accident this morning. Have you seen my cat anywhere?

seed   a tiny thing put into the ground so that a plant can grow from it

seek   to try to find
We sought for him everywhere, but could not find him.

seem   to make people think something is true or likely

seen   see see

see-saw   a plank balanced in the middle so that someone can sit on each end and make it go up and down

seize   to take hold of something suddenly
The cat seized the toy mouse.

seldom   not often
I seldom cry.

157

select to choose

self everything in a person that makes them different from anyone else

selfish only bothered about yourself and what you want

sell to give in return for money
I sold my bike yesterday.

semi-circle half of a circle
(See the list of shapes on p. 223)

semi-colon a mark like this ;

send to make a person or thing go somewhere
She sent me a card last week.

senior older or more important

sensation 1 anything that you can feel happening to yourself
The cold water gave me a tingling sensation in my feet.
2 something very exciting that happens

sense 1 the power to see, hear, smell, feel, or taste
2 the ability to know what it is best to do or say
She used her common sense and called an ambulance.

sensible wise
a sensible person
a sensible idea

sensitive easily hurt or offended
sensitive skin
a sensitive person

sent see **send**

sentence a group of words that belong together. A written sentence always begins with a capital letter and ends with a question mark like this ?, an exclamation mark like this !, or a full stop like this .
Is this a sentence? Yes, it is.

sentry a soldier who is guarding a building

separate not joined to anything

sequin one of the tiny, round, shiny things sewn on clothes to decorate them

sergeant a policeman or soldier who is in charge of other policemen or soldiers

serial a story told in parts
a television serial

series 1 a full set
a series of stamps
2 a number of things that are similar and come one after the other
a television series

serious 1 careful and thoughtful
a serious boy
2 not silly or funny
a serious talk
3 very bad
a serious accident

serpent a large snake

servant someone whose job is to work in someone else's house

serve 1 to work for someone
2 to sell things to people in a shop
3 to give food out at a meal

serviette a square of cloth or paper for keeping you clean while you eat

session a time spent doing one thing
We had a training session at the sports centre.

set 1 a group of people or things that belong together
a set of drums
2 to become solid or hard
The jelly has set very quickly.
3 to put
4 *to set off* to start
They set off for home.

settee   a long, comfortable seat with a back, for more than one person

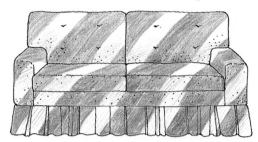

settle   **1** to get comfortable in a place and stay there
We're settling down in our new home now.
2 to decide
We've settled on the colour of the paint.

several   more than a few but not a lot

severe   **1** not kind or gentle
a severe teacher
2 very bad
a severe cold

sew   (*say* so)
to use a needle and cotton to join pieces of cloth together
He has sewn his badge on.

sex   one of the two groups, either male or female, that all people and animals belong to

shabby   looking worn and faded
shabby clothes

shack   a rough hut

shade   **1** a place that is darker and cooler than other places, because the light of the sun cannot get to it
2 how light or dark a colour is
3 to make part of a drawing darker than the rest

shadow   the dark shape that you see on the wall or ground near something that is standing in the way of the light

shaft   **1** a long, thin pole
the shaft of an arrow
2 a deep, narrow hole
a mine shaft

shaggy   with long, untidy hair
a shaggy dog

shake   to move quickly up and down or from side to side
I shook with fear when I saw it.
The trees were shaken by the wind.

shallow   not deep
shallow water

shame   the feeling you have when you are upset because you have done wrong

shameful   so bad that it brings you shame
shameful behaviour

shampoo   liquid soap used for washing hair

shape   the pattern that a line drawn round the outside of something makes. A ball has a round shape.

share   **1** to make something into parts and give them out to other people
She shared out the cake.
2 to use something that someone else is also using
Can I share your book?

shark   a large sea fish with sharp teeth

sharp **1** with an edge or point that can cut or make holes
a sharp knife
2 sudden
a sharp bend in the road
3 quick to notice things or learn
sharp eyes, a sharp boy

shatter to break suddenly into tiny pieces

shave to cut hair from the skin to make it smooth. Men shave their faces.

shawl a piece of cloth or knitting worn round the shoulders or wrapped round a baby

sheaf a bundle of corn stalks tied together at harvest time
three sheaves

shears a tool like a very large pair of scissors for cutting plants or grass, or for clipping wool from sheep

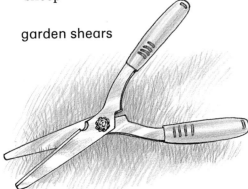

garden shears

sheath a cover for the sharp blade of a sword or knife

sheaves more than one **sheaf**

shed **1** a small hut
2 to let something fall. Trees shed leaves, people shed tears, and caterpillars shed their skins.

sheep an animal kept by farmers for its wool and meat
two sheep

sheer very steep because it is straight up and down like a wall
It was a sheer drop from the top of the cliff to the rocks below.

sheet **1** one of the large pieces of cloth put on a bed
2 a whole piece of paper, glass, or metal

shelf a long piece of wood fastened to a wall, for putting things on
two shelves

shell **1** the thin, hard part round an egg, a nut, and some kinds of animals, such as snails
2 a very large bullet that explodes when it hits something

shelter a place that protects people from wind, rain, cold, or danger
a bus shelter

shelves more than one **shelf**

shepherd someone whose job is to look after sheep

sheriff a man in charge of the law in a county or district

shield a large piece of metal, leather, or wood used for protecting someone. Soldiers long ago held shields in front of themselves while they were fighting.

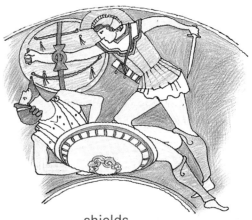

shields

shift   to move something
Help me shift the table.

shilling   a British coin that was worth the same as 5p.

shimmer   to shine with a light that comes and goes, like the light of the sun on water

shin   the front of the leg between the knee and ankle

shine   **1** to give out light
The sun shone all day.
2 to look very bright
He polished it until it shone.

shingle   a lot of small stones by the edge of the sea

shiny   with a surface that shines

ship   a large boat that takes people or things on long journeys over the sea   (See picture on p. 215)

shipwreck   a bad accident that destroys or sinks a ship while it is at sea

shirk   to get out of doing something that you ought to do
He was always shirking his turn to do the dishes.

shirt   a piece of clothing for the top half of the body with sleeves, a collar, and buttons down the front

shiver   to shake because you are cold or frightened

shoal   a large number of fish swimming together

shock   a big surprise that is not pleasant

shoe   a strong covering for the foot, with a stiff sole and heel
leather shoes

shone   see **shine**

shook   see **shake**

shoot   **1** to use a gun or a bow and arrow
2 to hurt or kill by shooting
A sheriff shot Billy the Kid.
3 to move very quickly
4 to kick, hit, or throw a ball at the goal
5 a part of a plant that has just grown

shop   **1** a place that people go into to buy things
2 to go to a shop to buy something

shore   the land along the edge of the sea

short   **1** not long
a short visit
2 not tall
a short person

shorthand   a set of signs for writing words down as quickly as people say them

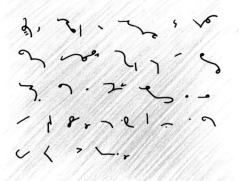

shorts   trousers that only cover the top part of the legs

shot   **1** see **shoot**
2 the firing of a gun

should   ought to
You should be working.

shoulder   the part of the body between the neck and arm

shout   to speak very loudly

shove   to push hard

shovel   a kind of curved spade for lifting things such as coal or sand

show   **1** to let something be seen
Show me your new bike.
2 to make something clear to someone
He's shown me how to do it.
3 singing, dancing, and acting done to entertain people
4 things that have been put together and arranged so that people can come and look at them
a flower show

shower   **1** a short fall of rain or snow
2 a lot of small things falling like rain
a shower of stones
3 *to have a shower* to stand under a spray of water and wash yourself

shown   see **show**

shrank   see **shrink**

shred   a tiny strip or piece that has been cut, broken, or torn off something

shriek   a short scream

shrill   sounding very high and loud
a shrill whistle

shrimp   a small sea creature with a shell

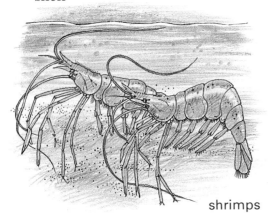

shrimps

shrink   to become smaller
It shrank when it was washed.
These jeans have shrunk.

shrivel   to get very dry and curl up at the edges like a dead leaf

shrub   a bush

shrunk   see **shrink**

shudder   to shake suddenly because you are very cold or frightened

shuffle   to drag your feet along the ground as you walk

shunt   to move a train on to a different line

shut   to move a cover, lid, or door in order to block up an opening

shutter   **1** a wooden cover that fits over a window
2 the part inside a camera that opens to let in light as you take a photograph

shutters (1)

shy   **1** not willing to meet other people because you are afraid
2 easily frightened
a shy animal

sick   **1** ill
2 *to be sick* to bring food back up from the stomach through the mouth

side 1 one of the outer parts between the front and back of a person, animal, or thing
2 a flat surface
A cube has six sides.
3 an edge
A triangle has three sides.
4 a group playing or fighting against another group

sideboard a long, heavy piece of furniture with drawers, cupboards, and a flat top where things can be put

sideways 1 with the side first
The piano will fit through the door if you carry it sideways.
2 to one side
He moved sideways to avoid the puddle.

siege (*say* seej)
a time when the enemy surrounds a town or castle so that people and things cannot get in or out

sigh to breathe out heavily to show you are feeling very sad or very happy

sight 1 the ability to see
You are lucky to have good sight.
2 something that is seen
He was a funny sight in that hat.

sign 1 anything written, drawn, or done to tell or show people something
road signs
2 to write your name in your own writing

signal a sound or movement that tells people something without words *traffic signals*

signature your name written by yourself in your own writing

silence a time when there is no sound at all

silent without any sound

silk very fine, shiny cloth made from threads spun by insects called **silk-worms**

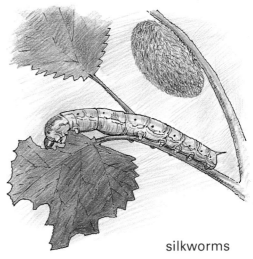

silkworms

sill a ledge underneath a window

silly not clever or careful
a silly person, a silly idea

silver a valuable, shiny white metal

similar like another person or thing
Your dress is similar to mine.

simple 1 easy
a simple question
2 plain
a simple dress
3 not complicated

since 1 from that time
We have been friends since last summer.
2 because
An outing was not organized since few people wanted to go.

sincere truly meant
sincere good wishes

sing to use the voice to make a tune with sounds or words
We have sung this before.
She sang a solo yesterday.

singe to burn something slightly

single **1** only one
The tree has a single apple.
2 not married

sink **1** a place with taps where you do the washing-up
2 to go under water
The ship sank last night.
It has sunk.
3 to go down

sip to drink a very small amount at a time

sir **1** a word used when speaking politely to a man, instead of his name
2 a title given to knights
Sir Winston Churchill

siren a machine that makes a loud sound like a scream to warn people about something

sister a girl or woman who has the same parents as another person

sit to rest on your bottom, as you do when you are on a chair
She sat on the chair and broke it.
Are you sitting comfortably?

site the ground where something has been built or will be built

situation **1** the place where something is
2 the things that are happening to you

size **1** how big something is
2 the measurement something is made in
size ten shoes

sizzle to make the noise sausages make when they are being fried

skate **1** a steel blade joined to the sole of a boot and used for moving smoothly over ice
2 to move smoothly over ice or the ground wearing skates or roller-skates

skateboard a long piece of wood or plastic on wheels. You balance on it with both feet while it moves quickly over the ground.

skeleton the framework of bones inside the body

sketch **1** to draw quickly
2 a quick or rough drawing

ski a long piece of metal and plastic strapped to the foot for moving quickly and smoothly over snow
a pair of skis

a skier

ski

skid to slide without meaning to
The car skidded on the wet road surface.

skill the ability to do something very well

skim 1 to take the cream off the top of milk
2 to move quickly over the surface of something and only just touch it

skin 1 the outer covering of the body
2 the outer covering of some fruits and vegetables

skip 1 to move lightly and quickly by hopping from one foot to the other
2 to jump over a rope that is turning
3 to miss out
Skip the next page.

skipper the person in charge of a ship or a team

skirt a piece of clothing for women and girls that hangs down from the waist

skittle one of a set of pieces of wood or plastic shaped like bottles that people try to knock down with a ball

skull the bony framework inside the head

sky the space overhead where the sun, moon, and stars can be seen

skylark a small, brown bird that sings while flying high in the air

skyscraper a very tall, modern building

slab a flat, thick piece
a slab of toffee

slack 1 not pulled tight
a slack rope
2 careless
slack work
3 not busy
a slack day

slain see **slay**

slam to close something loudly

slanting in a line that is higher at one end than the other, like the side of a triangle or a hill

slap to hit with the flat part of your hand

slash to make long cuts in something

slate one of the thin pieces of smooth, grey rock used to cover a roof

slaughter the killing of many people or animals

slave someone who belongs to another person and has to work without wages

slay to kill
The dragon was slain.
St. George slew the dragon.

sled, sledge something used for travelling over snow with strips of metal or wood, or a smooth base, instead of wheels

sleek neat, smooth, and shiny

sleep to close your eyes and rest completely, as you do every night
I slept in a tent last night.

sleet a mixture of rain and snow

sleeve the part of a coat, shirt, blouse, or jersey, that covers the arm

sleigh (*rhymes with* play) something used for travelling over snow. Sleighs are pulled by animals and have strips of wood or metal instead of wheels.

slender thin
a slender girl

slept see **sleep**

slew see **slay**

slide 1 to move very quickly and smoothly over something
2 very slippery ground or a long, sloping piece of shiny metal that people can slide on
3 something pretty that girls put in their hair to keep it tidy
4 a small photograph that can be shown on a screen

slight 1 small
a slight cold
2 thin
a very slight person

slim 1 thin
2 to try to get thinner by eating less
My father is slimming.

slime wet, slippery stuff that is not pleasant

sling 1 a piece of cloth wrapped round an injured arm and tied round the neck so that it supports the arm
2 a short leather strap used for throwing stones

slink to move in a secret way because you are afraid or feel guilty about something
The dog saw me watching and slunk away.

slip 1 slide out of place
2 to fall over
He slipped on some ice.
3 to go away quickly and quietly
She slipped out of the room when the baby fell asleep.

slipper a soft, comfortable kind of shoe worn indoors

slippery with a very smooth surface so that it is difficult to get hold of or walk on

slit a long cut or a narrow opening in something

slop to make a mess by letting liquid run over the edge of a container
The bucket was so full that some water slopped out.

slope 1 ground that is like the side of a hill
It's hard to run up a steep slope.
2 to be slanting
Does the roof slope or is it flat?

slot a narrow opening for something like a coin to fit into
Put a coin in the slot and you'll get a ticket.

slouch to move, sit, or stand with the head and shoulders bent forwards
The tired pupil slouched at his desk.

slow 1 taking more time than usual
a slow train
2 showing a time that is earlier than the correct time. Watches and clocks are sometimes slow.

sludge thick, sticky mud

slug a small creature like a snail without its shell

slum an area of old, dirty, crowded houses

slumber sleep

slunk see **slink**

slush melting snow

sly clever at tricking people secretly

smack to hit with the flat part of the hand

small little
a small dog

smart 1 dressed well
That hat looks very smart.
2 neat and tidy
If you comb your hair, you'll look much smarter.
3 clever
What a smart dog!
4 to feel a stinging pain
The bee sting made his hand smart.

smash to break into pieces with a loud noise

smear 1 to make a dirty mark by rubbing against something
2 to rub something over a surface

smell 1 to use the nose to find out about something
I bent down and smelt the rose.
2 anything that can be smelt

smile to make your face show that you are happy

smith someone who makes things out of metal

smoke 1 blue or grey gas that floats up from a fire and looks like a cloud
2 to have a cigarette or pipe between the lips, take in the smoke from it, and breathe it out

smooth free from lumps or rough parts
a smooth surface

smother 1 to cover thickly
a cake smothered in cream
2 to cover someone's mouth and nose so that they cannot breathe

smoulder to burn slowly with a lot of smoke

smudge a dirty mark made by rubbing against something

smuggle to bring something into a country secretly without paying the tax that should be paid to the government

snack something you can eat quickly instead of a meal

snail a small creature that lives inside a shell. Snails are found on land and in water.

snails

snake a creature with a long body and no legs. Some snakes can give poisonous bites.

snap **1** to break suddenly
2 to bite suddenly
The horse snapped at his groom.

snapshot a photograph

snare a trap for catching animals

snarl to make the sound a dog makes when it is angry

snatch to take something quickly

sneak **1** someone who tells tales
2 to move trying not to be seen or heard
She sneaked up behind him and made him jump.

sneer to speak or smile in an insulting way that shows that you think someone is not worth bothering about

sneeze to make a sudden noise as air rushes out of the nose
I can't stop sneezing.

sniff to make a noise by suddenly taking in air through the nose

snip to cut a little bit off something

snob someone who only bothers with people that they think are clever or important

snooker a game played on a long table with rods and twenty-two small, coloured balls

snore to breathe very noisily while sleeping

snorkel a tube for someone to breathe through while they are swimming under water

snorkel

snout an animal's nose and mouth sticking out from the rest of its face. Pigs have snouts.

snow small, thin, white flakes of frozen water. Snow floats down from the sky when the weather is very cold.

snowdrop a small white flower that grows in January and February (See picture on p. 218)

snub to show someone who is trying to be friendly that you do not want to be their friend

snug cosy

snuggle to curl up in a warm, comfortable place
The kitten snuggled up to its mother.

soak to make something very wet

soap something used with water for washing

soar to move high into the air
The eagle soared high above them.

sock a covering for the foot and part of the leg

socket   the part that an electric light bulb or plug fits into

sofa   a long, comfortable seat with a back, for more than one person

soft   1 not firm. Cotton wool and wet clay are soft.
2 not loud

software   the programs that are put into a computer

soggy   wet through

soil   the brown stuff on the ground, that plants grow in

solar   anything to do with the sun
solar energy, the solar system

sold   see **sell**

soldier   a member of the army

sole   1 the flat part underneath a foot or shoe
2 a sea fish that is eaten
(See picture on p. 220)

solemn   serious

solid   1 not hollow. A cricket ball is solid. A tennis ball is not.
2 firm. Liquids and gases are not solid.
solid rock

solitary   alone or lonely

solo   something sung, played, danced, or done by one person

solution   1 the answer to a puzzle or problem
2 something dissolved in a liquid

solve   to find the answer to a puzzle

some   1 a few
some sweets
2 a certain amount of
some cake
3 a, an, or one
Some insect has just bitten me.

somebody   a person

somehow   in some way

someone   a person

somersault   (*say* summer-solt)
1 a jump, turning head over heels in the air
2 a forward or backward roll on the ground

something   some thing

sometimes   at some times

somewhere   in some place or to some place

son   a boy or man who is someone's child

song   words that are sung

soon   in a very short time from now

soot   the black powder left behind by smoke

soothe   to make someone who is upset feel calm
soothing words

sorcerer   a man in fairy tales, who can do magic things

sore   painful when it is touched
sore skin

sorrow   a very sad feeling

sorry **1** sad about something that you wish you had not done
2 sad because of something that has happened to another person

sort **1** a kind
I like this sort best.
2 to arrange things into different groups

sought see **seek**

soul the part of a person that cannot be seen but is believed to go on living after they have died

sound **1** anything that can be heard
2 to make a sound

soup a hot liquid made from meat or vegetables

sour **1** with the kind of taste lemons and vinegar have
2 not fresh
sour milk

source the place something has come from
The source of the river is up in the hills.

south the direction to your right when you face east

southern from the south or in the south

souvenir (*say* soo-ven-eer) something that you keep because it makes you think about a person or place
He brought back souvenirs from his holiday.

sovereign a ruler who is a king, queen, emperor, or empress

sow¹ (*rhymes with* toe) to put seeds in the ground so that they will grow into plants
The grain was sown in the spring.

sow² (*rhymes with* how) a female pig

space **1** the distance between things
2 a place with nothing in it
3 all the places beyond the earth, where the stars and planets are. Outer space is so vast that it cannot be measured.

spacecraft any kind of vehicle that can travel in space

spaceship a machine that can carry people and things through space

space shuttle a spaceship designed to carry people and cargo from earth to a satellite and back

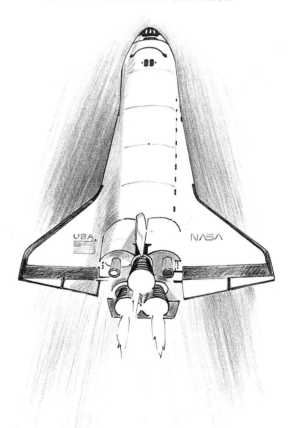

spade **1** a tool with a long handle and a short, wide blade for digging **2** a small, black spade printed on some playing-cards (See picture on p. 222)

spaghetti a food that looks like long pieces of string when it is cooked

span **1** to reach from one side of something to the other, as a bridge does
2 the distance between the top of the thumb and the top of the little finger when the hand is spread out

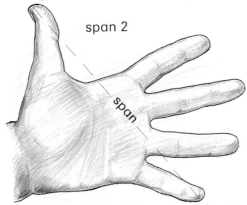

span 2

spaniel a kind of dog with silky fur and long ears (See picture on p. 220)

spank to hit someone hard on the bottom

spanner a tool that fits round a nut so that you can turn it to make it tighter or looser

spare **1** not used but kept in case it is needed
a spare tyre
2 to give up something so that someone else can have it
Could you spare one of your pencils?

spark **1** a tiny piece of burning stuff **2** a tiny flash

sparkle to shine with a lot of tiny flashes of bright light

sparkler a kind of firework that sparkles. You can hold it in your hand while it burns.

sparklers

sparrow a small, brown bird that is often seen in gardens

spat see **spit**

spawn the eggs of frogs, fish, and some other water creatures
We saw some frog spawn in the pond.

speak to say something
She spoke to me yesterday.
I've not spoken to him yet.

spear a long pole or stick with a very sharp point, used as a weapon

special **1** different from any other kind
2 for one person or thing
a special cake for my birthday

specimen **1** a small amount of something that shows what the rest is like
2 an example of one kind of plant or animal
She showed them a specimen of an oak leaf.

speck **1** a tiny mark
2 a tiny bit of dust

speckled with small, coloured spots. Some birds' eggs are speckled.

spectacles a pair of glasses

spectator someone watching a game or show

speech **1** the power of speaking
2 a talk given to a group of people
The headmaster made a speech to the parents.

speed how quickly something moves or happens

spell **1** to write a word correctly
How is your name spelt?
2 magic words that make things happen

spend **1** to use money to pay for things
2 to pass time
I spent yesterday at home.

sphere (*say* sfear)
the shape of a ball
(See the list of shapes on p. 223)

spice part of a plant such as the berry or seed that is dried and used in cooking to give food a stronger flavour. Ginger and pepper are spices.

spider a small creature with eight legs that sometimes weaves webs to catch insects

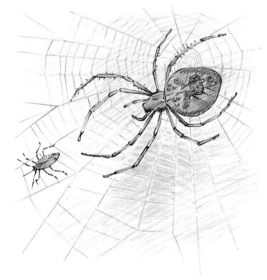

spike a thin piece of metal with a sharp point

spill to let something fall out of a container
The cat drank the spilt milk.

spin **1** to turn round and round quickly
I spun round until I was dizzy.
2 to make thread by twisting long, thin pieces of wool or cotton together

spinach (*say* spin-itch)
a vegetable with a lot of green leaves, which you cook to eat

spine **1** the long bone down the centre of your back
2 a thorn or prickle

spinning-wheel a machine for spinning thread. It is worked by the hand or foot.

spinster a woman who has not married

spiral **1** the shape of a line that keeps going round the same point in smaller and smaller or bigger and bigger curves, like the jam in a slice of Swiss roll
(See the list of shapes on p. 222)
2 *a spiral staircase* a staircase that you go round and round as you climb up it

spire a tall, pointed part on top of a church tower

spirit **1** the part of a person that cannot be seen but is believed to go on living after they have died
2 a ghost
3 something that makes a person very brave and lively
He was in high spirits on the morning of the race.

spit to send drops of liquid out of the mouth
The cat spat when it saw the dog.

spiteful full of a wish to hurt someone by what you say or do

splash **1** to make drops of water fly about as they do when you jump into water
2 the noise you make when you jump into water

splendid **1** very good
a splendid holiday
2 looking very grand
a splendid uniform

splint a straight piece of wood or metal that is tied to a broken arm or leg to hold it firm

splinter a sharp bit of wood, glass, or metal

split to break something into parts

spoil **1** to make something less good or useful than it was
The ink stain has spoilt my dress.
2 to be too kind to a child so that they think they can always have what they want
The little boy was very spoilt.

spoke **1** see **speak**
2 one of the wires or rods that go from the centre of a wheel to the rim

spoken see **speak**

sponge **1** a light, soft cake
2 something thick and soft with a lot of holes in it. Sponges soak up water and are used for washing.

sponsor someone who gives money to a charity for something done by another person

spool a round piece of wood or metal that cotton, string, or film is wound round

spoon what you use for eating soup and pudding

sport a game or something else that is usually done outside and exercises the body. Running, jumping, football, and netball are all sports.

spot **1** a round mark
2 a small, round swelling on the skin
3 a place
This is a good spot for a picnic.
4 to notice something
She spotted the mistake at once.

spotlight a strong light that can shine on one small area

spout the part of a container that is made like a pipe so that you can pour liquid out of it easily. Teapots and kettles have spouts.

sprain to twist the wrist or ankle so that it swells and is painful

sprang see **spring**

sprawl to sit or lie with your arms and legs spread out

spray to make tiny drops of liquid fall all over something

spread **1** to stretch something out to its full size
The bird spread its wings.
2 to make something cover a surface
She spread the cloth on the table.

spring   **1** the part of the year when plants start to grow and the days are getting lighter and warmer
2 a place where water comes out of the ground
3 a piece of metal wound into rings so that it jumps back into shape after it has been pressed or stretched
4 to move suddenly upwards
I sprang up and caught the ball.
Weeds had sprung up everywhere.

sprinkle   to make a few tiny pieces or drops fall on something

sprint   to run a short distance very quickly

sprout   **1** to start to grow
The seeds soon sprouted.
2 a vegetable that looks like a tiny cabbage
Brussels sprouts

sprung   see **spring**

spun   see **spin**

spurt   **1** to move like water shooting suddenly upwards
The water spurted out of the broken pipe.
2 to go faster suddenly

spy   **1** someone who works secretly to find out things about another person or country
2 to notice
I spy with my little eye . . .

squabble   to quarrel about something that is not important

square   a flat shape with four straight sides that are all the same length
(See the list of shapes on p. 223)

squash   **1** to press something hard so that it goes out of shape
2 a drink made from fruit
3 a game played indoors with rackets and a small rubber ball

squat   to sit on the ground with your knees bent and your bottom resting on your heels

squaw   a female American Indian

squeak   to make the tiny, shrill sound a mouse makes

squeal   to make a long, shrill sound
The pig squealed as it ran.

squeeze   to press something between your hands or two other things

squid   a sea creature with eight short arms and two very long ones

squirm   to twist and turn the body about, like a worm
He squirmed to avoid his aunt's kiss.

squirrel   a small animal with a very thick tail that lives in trees

squirt   to come or squeeze suddenly out of something
Too much toothpaste squirted out.
He squirted washing-up liquid into the water.

stab   to hit someone with the sharp, pointed end of a knife or sword

stable   a building in which horses are kept

stack   a neat pile

stadium   a large place where people can watch sports and games

staff   1 a group of people who work together in an office, shop, or school
2 a thick stick for walking with

stag   a male deer

stage   1 a raised floor in a hall or theatre, on which people act, sing, or dance to entertain other people
2 the point someone has reached in doing something
The baby is at the crawling stage.

stagger   to try to stand or walk but find it difficult to stay upright

stagnant   not flowing or fresh
a pool of stagnant water

stain   a dirty mark made on something by liquid

stair   one of a set of steps for going up or down inside a building

staircase   a set of stairs and banisters

stake   a thick, pointed stick
She used a stake to support the rose bush.

stale   not fresh
stale bread

stalk   1 a thin stem
2 to walk in a stiff way that shows you are angry
She stalked away from the game.
3 to move secretly to get close to an animal you are hunting

stall   1 a kind of small shop or a table that things are sold on. Markets have stalls.
2 a place for one animal in a stable or shed

stallion   a male horse.

stammer   to keep repeating the sounds at the beginning of words when you speak

stamp   1 to bang the foot heavily on the ground
2 a piece of sticky paper with a picture on it. People put stamps on letters and parcels to show that they have paid to post them.

stand   1 to be on your feet without moving
I stood there until they came.
2 something made for putting things on
a cake stand, a hat stand

standard   1 how good something is
a high standard of work
2 a flag

stank   see **stink**

stapler   a small machine that fastens papers together by pressing little pieces of wire into them

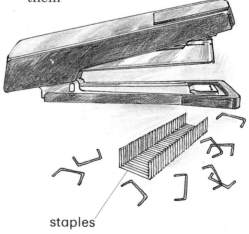

staples

star   1 one of the tiny, bright lights you see in the sky at night
2 a famous singer or actor

starch   part of the food we eat, especially potatoes. It can be made into a powder or liquid and used for making clothes stiff.

stare   to look at someone or something for a long time, without moving your eyes

starling   a dark brown bird often seen in large flocks

starlings

start   **1** to take the first steps in doing something
She has started going to Brownies.
2 to make something happen
They have started a chess club at school.

startle   to make a person or animal very surprised and frightened
startling news

starvation   illness or death caused by great hunger

starve   to be very ill or die because you have not got enough food

state   **1** how someone or something is
His clothes were in a dreadful state.
2 to say something important
The policeman stated that he saw the man steal the watch.
3 a country or part of a country
United States of America

statement   words that say something important

station   **1** a place where people get on or off trains
2 a building for policemen or firemen

statue   a model of a person made in stone or metal

stay   **1** to be in the same place
2 to live somewhere as a visitor

steady   not shaking in any way
a steady voice, a steady hand

steak   (*rhymes with* rake)
a thick slice of meat or fish

steal   to take something that does not belong to you and keep it
A dog stole the meat yesterday.
The jewels were stolen.

steam   very hot water that has turned into a vapour

steel   a strong, shiny metal made from iron

steep   sloping sharply
a steep hill

steeple   a tall, pointed tower on top of a church

steer   to make a ship, car, or bicycle go in the direction you want

stem   **1** the main part of a plant above the ground
2 the thin part that joins a leaf, flower, or fruit to the rest of the plant

step   **1** the movement you make with your foot when you are walking, running, or dancing
2 a flat place where you can put your foot when you are going up or down something

stepfather   a man who is married to your mother but is not your real father

stepmother   a woman who is married to your father but is not your real mother

stern   **1** the back end of a boat (See picture on p. 215)
2 severe or strict
The headmaster looked very stern.

stew 1 meat and vegetables cooked in liquid
2 to cook something slowly in liquid

stick 1 a long, thin piece of wood
2 a long, thin piece of anything
a stick of liquorice
3 to become fastened or joined to things, as glue and mud do
The sweets were stuck to the bag.
4 to press a sharp point into something
Stick a pin in the balloon and it will burst.

sticky able to stick to things. Glue, jam, and honey are all sticky.

stiff not easily bent
stiff cardboard

stile a set of steps made to help people get over a fence

stile

still 1 not moving
Hold it still.
2 the same now as before
He is still ill.

stilts a pair of poles with which you can walk high above the ground

sting 1 a sharp part with poison on it that some animals and plants have
A nettle sting hurts.
2 to hurt someone with a sting
A bee stung me yesterday.

stink to have a very strong, bad smell
The stable was filthy and stank.
It has always stunk like this.

stir 1 to move a liquid or a soft mixture round with a spoon
He stirred the cake mixture.
2 to start to move
After a long sleep the baby started to stir.

stirrup the metal part that hangs down each side of a horse's saddle for you to put your foot in while you are riding

stitch 1 a loop of thread made by the needle in sewing
2 one of the loops of wool on a knitting needle
3 a sudden pain in the side. People sometimes get stitches when they have been running.

stoat a small, brown, furry animal with a long body that kills and eats mice, rats, birds, and rabbits

stock 1 a lot of things kept ready to be sold or used
This shop is selling old stock cheaply.
2 a garden flower with a sweet smell

stocking a covering for the foot and leg worn next to the skin

stoke to put coal or wood on a fire to keep it burning

stole, stolen   see **steal**

stomach   the part in the middle of the body, where food goes when it is eaten

stone   **1** rock
2 a small piece of rock
3 the hard seed in the middle of a cherry, plum, peach, or apricot
4 a measure for weight
She weighs 4 stone.

stood   see **stand**

stool   a small seat without a back

stoop   to bend the body forwards

stop   **1** to end
At last the baby stopped crying.
2 to come to rest
The bus stopped.
3 to stay

stopper   something that fits into the top of a bottle to close it

store   **1** to keep things until they are needed
The spare pencils were stored in the cupboard.
2 a large shop
This store sells everything.

storey   all the rooms on the same floor in a building

stork   a large bird with very long legs and a long beak

storm   a very strong wind with a lot of rain or snow

story   words that tell you about something that has really happened or about something that someone has made up
adventure stories

stout   fat
a stout lady

stove   something that gives out heat for warming a room or for cooking

straight   **1** like a line drawn with a ruler
a straight road
2 *straight away* at once

straighten   **1** to make something straight
2 to become straight

strain   **1** to stretch, push, or try too hard
2 to hurt part of yourself by stretching or pushing too hard
The football player strained his ankle.
3 to separate a liquid from lumps or other things floating in it. People strain tea to get rid of the tea leaves.

strange   **1** not known or seen before
a strange place
2 unusual and very surprising
a strange story

stranger   **1** someone in a place he does not know
2 someone you do not know

strangle   to kill someone by pressing on their throat until they cannot breathe

strap   a flat strip of leather or another strong material for fastening things together

straw   **1** dry stalks of corn
2 a very thin tube for drinking through

strawberry a small, red, juicy fruit
strawberry jam

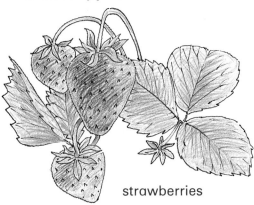

strawberries

stray lost and without a home
a stray cat

streak **1** a long, narrow mark
The tears made streaks down her dirty face.
2 to move very quickly
The jet streaked across the sky.

stream a small river

streamer a long strip of paper or a ribbon joined by one end to something to decorate it

street a road with houses along each side

strength how strong someone or something is

stretch to pull something to make it longer, wider, or tighter

stretcher a pair of poles with canvas stretched across them for carrying a sick or injured person

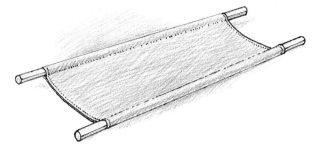

strict keen on always being obeyed
strict parents

stride to walk with long steps
I strode angrily out of the room.

strike **1** to hit
The house was struck by lightning.
2 *to strike a match* to rub a match along something rough so that it bursts into flame
3 to stop working until the people in charge agree to make things better
The women voted to strike for better working conditions.

string very thin rope

strip **1** a long, narrow piece
She cut off a strip of paper.
2 to take off clothes or a covering
He stripped off his clothes and jumped in the bath.

stripe a coloured band across or down something

strode see **stride**

stroke **1** to move the hand gently along something
2 a hitting movement
We learnt a new tennis stroke.

stroll to walk slowly, because you are enjoying your walk and do not have to get anywhere

strong **1** healthy and able to do things that need a lot of energy
a strong horse
2 not easily broken
strong rope
3 with a lot of flavour
strong tea

struck see **strike**

structure **1** anything that has been built
2 the way something has been built
The structure of the human body is very complicated.

struggle **1** to use your arms and legs in fighting or trying to get free
The thief struggled to get away from the police.
2 to try very hard to do something you find difficult
He struggled to improve his football skills.

stubborn not willing to change your ideas even though they might be wrong

stuck see **stick**

stud a small knob like the ones on the sole of a football boot

student someone who studies at college or university

studio a place where films, or radio, or television programmes are made

study **1** to spend time learning about something
We studied space travel in our project.
2 to look at something very carefully
He studied the map, looking for the place.
3 a room where someone studies
The book is in the study.

stuff **1** anything used for making things
2 to fill something tightly
3 to push something inside another thing

stuffy without fresh air
a stuffy room

stumble to fall over something

stump **1** the part of a broken tree, tooth, or pencil that is left
2 one of the set of three upright sticks put at each end of the pitch in cricket

stump 1

stun **1** to hit or hurt someone so much that they cannot think properly
2 to make someone very surprised
She was stunned to receive so many presents.

stung see **sting**

stunk see **stink**

stupid **1** very silly
a stupid idea
2 slow to learn and understand

sturdy strong and healthy
a sturdy child

stutter to keep repeating the sounds at the beginning of words when you speak

sty **1** a sore swelling on the edge of an eyelid
2 a place where pigs are kept
two sties

style the way something is done or made
That is a neat style of writing.

subject **1** the person or thing that you are writing about or learning about
What is the subject of your project?
2 someone who is ruled by a king, queen, or government
We are all subjects of the Queen.

submarine a ship that can travel under water

substance anything that can be seen, touched, or used for making things
Glue is a sticky substance.

subtract to find the answer to a sum like this 6 − 3 =

subway a tunnel made under the ground so that people can get to the other side of a road safely

succeed to do or get what you wanted to do or get
She succeeded in winning the race.

successful able to do or get what you wanted to do or get

such **1** of the same kind
sweets such as these
2 so great
It was such a surprise!

suck **1** to take in air or liquid from something
I sucked milk through a straw.
2 to keep moving something around inside your mouth without chewing it
He sucked a sweet.

sudden happening quickly without any warning
a sudden scream

suede (*say* swade)
a kind of soft leather that is not shiny

suet (*say* soo-it)
hard fat that comes from sheep and cattle and is used in cooking

suffer to have to put up with pain or something else that is not pleasant

sufficient enough

sugar a sweet food that is put in drinks and other foods to make them taste sweet

suggest to give someone an idea that you think is useful

suit **1** a jacket and a pair of trousers or skirt that are meant to be worn together
2 to fit in with someone's plans
Does it suit you if we start at once?
3 to look well on someone
That colour suits you.

suitable just right for something
suitable shoes for dancing

suitcase a kind of box with a lid and a handle for carrying clothes and other things on journeys

suite (*say* sweet)
a set of furniture

sulk to stop speaking to your friends, because you are angry about something

sultana a dried grape

summer the hottest part of the year

summit the top of a mountain

sun the star that gives the earth heat and light

sundial a kind of clock that uses a shadow made by the sun to show what time it is

sung see **sing**

sunk see **sink**

sunny with the sun shining
a sunny day

sunrise the time when the sun rises

sunset the time when the sun goes down

sunshine the light and heat that come from the sun when it is shining

supermarket a large shop where people help themselves to things as they go round and pay for them all on the way out

supersonic faster than sound travels
a supersonic aeroplane

supper a meal or snack eaten in the evening

supply 1 to give what is needed
The school supplies all our pencils.
2 things kept ready to be used when needed
a supply of paper

support 1 to hold up something so that it does not fall
2 to give help to someone

suppose to think something is true although it might not be

sure knowing something is true or right
I'm sure her name is Mary.

surface 1 the part all round the outside of something
2 the top of a table or desk

surgeon a doctor who is trained to do operations

surgery the room you go in to see a doctor or dentist

surname your last name that is the same as your family's name

surprise 1 the feeling you have when something suddenly happens that you were not expecting
To her surprise, she saw a cow in her garden.
2 something that happens and was not expected

surrender to stop fighting and agree to obey the enemy

surround to be all round someone or something
The playground is surrounded by a fence.

suspect to have a feeling that there might be something wrong

suspicious   feeling that there might be something wrong

swallow   **1** to make something go down your throat
2 a bird with a dark blue body, a long tail, and pointed wings

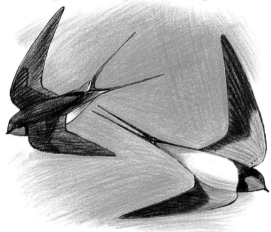

swallows (2)

swam   see **swim**

swamp   an area of very wet ground

swan   a big white bird with a very long neck that lives on water or near to it

swap   (*rhymes with* hop) to change one thing for another thing

swarm   a large number of insects together
a swarm of bees

sway   to move from side to side

swear   **1** to make a very serious promise
He has sworn to tell the truth.
2 to use bad words
He swore when he hit his finger.

sweat   to lose liquid through your skin, because you are ill or very hot
He was sweating after running the race.

sweater   a jersey

sweep   **1** to use a brush to clear away dust and litter from something
I swept this floor yesterday.
2 someone whose job is to clean chimneys

sweet   **1** with the taste of sugar or honey
2 very pleasant
a sweet smell
3 a small piece of sweet food made of sugar or chocolate
a bag of sweets
4 a pudding

swell   to get bigger
My broken ankle has swollen.

swelling   a swollen place on the body

swept   see **sweep**

swerve   to move suddenly to one side so that you will not bump into something

swift   **1** quick
2 a bird with long wings that flies very quickly

swift 2

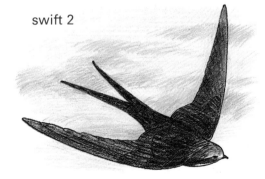

swill   the food and liquid given to pigs

swim   **1** to move the body through water, without touching the bottom
I swam a length yesterday.
2 to cross water by swimming
She has swum the Channel.

swindle to make someone believe something that is not true in order to get something valuable from them

swing 1 to move backwards and forwards, from side to side, or in a curve
The door swung open in the wind.
2 a seat hung from a tree or metal bar so that it can move backwards and forwards

swipe to hit hard
He swiped at the ball and it went over the fence.

swirl to move around quickly in circles
The water swirled down the drain.

switch 1 anything that is turned or pressed in order to make something work or stop working
an electric light switch
2 to change from one thing to another
She switched from ballet to tap-dancing.

swollen see **swell**

swoop to fly down suddenly to attack something

sword (*say* sord)
a weapon like a knife with a very long blade

swore, sworn see **swear**

swum see **swim**

swung see **swing**

sycamore a kind of large tree. Its seeds have wings and so they can be carried a long way by the wind. (See picture on p. 219)

syllable any word or part of a word that has one separate sound when you say it. *Bi-cy-cle* has three syllables and *bike* has one syllable.

symmetrical with two halves that are exactly alike but the opposite way round. Butterflies, spectacles, and wheels are symmetrical.

sympathy the feeling you have when you are sorry for someone who is sad, ill, or in trouble, and want to help them

synagogue a building where Jews worship

syrup a very sweet, sticky, liquid

system a set of parts, things, or ideas that work together
In London there is an underground railway system.

T t

tabby 1 a grey or brown cat with dark stripes in its fur
2 a female cat

table 1 a piece of furniture with a flat top and legs
2 a list of facts arranged in order

table-cloth a piece of material spread over a table to cover it

tablet a small, solid piece of medicine

tack 1 a short nail with a flat top
2 to sew two pieces of material together quickly, with long stitches

tackle 1 to try to do a job that needs doing
We must tackle the mess in the garage.
2 to try to get the ball from someone else in a football game
3 all the things needed for doing something
fishing tackle

tadpole a tiny creature that lives in water and will turn into a frog, toad, or newt

tail   the part at the end of something. Most animals have tails and so do aeroplanes.

tailor   someone whose job is to make suits and coats

take   **1** to get hold of something
He took his prize and smiled.
2 to carry or lead away
The money was taken yesterday.
Dad is taking us to the zoo.

take-away   a place where you can buy cooked food to take away

tale   a story

talent   the ability to do something very well
a talent for singing

talk   to speak to other people

talkative   fond of talking

tall   measuring more than usual from top to bottom
a tall person, a tall tree

tambourine   a musical instrument that you shake or hit with your fingers

tame   not wild or dangerous. Tame animals can be kept as pets, because they are not frightened of people.

tamper   to make changes in something so that it will not work properly

tan   **1** skin that has gone brown because of the sun
a sun-tan
2 light brown
a tan-coloured suitcase
3 to make the skin of an animal into leather
The man was tanning the seal skin.

tangerine   a kind of small orange

tangled   twisted up in knots
tangled wool, tangled hair

tank   **1** a large container for liquid. Fish tanks are made of glass and hot water tanks are made of metal.
2 a kind of very strong, heavy car used in war. It has a big gun on top and two long strips of metal round its wheels so that it can move over rough ground.

tanker   **1** a large ship for carrying oil
2 a large lorry for carrying milk or petrol

tanker 1

tanker 2

tape   **1** a narrow strip of cotton used in tying things and making loops or labels for clothes
name tapes
2 a narrow strip of special plastic used in a tape-recorder
cassette tape

taper to get very narrow at one end

tape-recorder a machine for recording on tape and playing it back

tapestry a piece of strong cloth covered with stitches that make a picture

tar a thick, black, sticky liquid made from coal or wood and used for making roads

target something that people aim at and try to hit

tart 1 pastry with jam or fruit on it 2 very sour. Rhubarb without sugar tastes tart.

tartan Scottish woollen cloth woven with a check pattern and used for making kilts

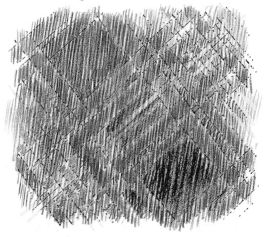

task a piece of work that must be done

tassel a bundle of threads tied together at the top and used to decorate things

taste 1 to eat a little bit of food or sip a drink to see what it is like 2 the flavour something has when you taste it

tasty with a strong, pleasant taste *tasty kippers*

tattered badly torn *The slippers were tattered after the puppy chewed them.*

taught see **teach**

tax money that people have to give to the government

taxi a car that you can travel in if you pay the driver *two taxis*

tea 1 a hot drink made with boiling water and the dried leaves of a **tea-plant** 2 a meal eaten in the afternoon

teach to make someone else able to understand or do something *She taught me to swim last year.*

teacher someone whose job is to teach

team a group of people who work together or play together on the same side in a game

teapot a kind of jug with a spout and lid, used for making tea

tear[1] (*rhymes with* fear) a small drop of water that comes out of the eye when you cry

tear[2] (*rhymes with* fair) to pull something apart so that you damage it *I tore the letter up and threw it away.* *His coat was torn.*

tease to bother or annoy someone for fun

teem 1 to rain very hard 2 to be full of moving things *The river was teeming with fish.*

teenager someone who is between thirteen and nineteen years old

teeth more than one tooth

telegram a short message that the post office sends very quickly

telegraph **1** to send a telegram
2 *telegraph pole* a tall pole that holds up telephone wires

telephone **1** an instrument that makes sound travel along wires so that you can speak to someone far away
2 to use a telephone to speak to someone

telescope a tube with lenses at each end. People look through telescopes in order to see things that are far away.

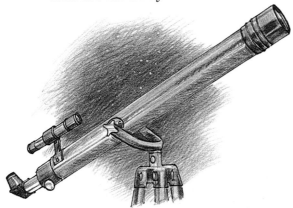

television a machine that picks up programmes sent through the air and changes them into pictures and sound so that people can watch them

tell to speak in order to pass on news, a story, or instructions
I told you about it yesterday.

temper **1** the mood someone is in
in a good temper
in a bad temper
2 *to lose your temper* to become very angry

temperature how hot or cold something is
They measured the temperature in the classroom.

temple a place where some people worship

temporary for a short time only
They were in a temporary classroom while their own was being decorated.

tempt to try to make someone do wrong
The gang tempted him to steal.

temptation something that makes you want to do wrong
The money on the desk was a temptation to the thief.

tend **1** to be likely to do something
He tends to fall asleep after dinner.
2 to look after
His grandfather tends the allotment.

tender **1** loving
a tender smile
2 soft
tender meat
3 sore
tender skin

tennis a game played by two or four people with rackets and a ball on a court with a net across the middle

tent a kind of shelter made of canvas stretched over poles. People sleep in tents when they are camping.

tents

187

tepid   only just warm
tepid water

term   the time between the main holidays, when school is open. There are three school terms in a year.

terminus   a place where a bus or train stops at the end of its journey

terrace   **1** a row of houses that are joined together
2 one of the set of stone steps where people stand to watch football matches
the terraces

terrapin   a creature that lives in water and looks like a small tortoise

terrible   very bad
terrible weather

terrier   a kind of small dog (See picture on p. 220)

terrific   **1** very good
a terrific idea
2 very big
a terrific idea

terrify   to make a person or animal very frightened
The rabbit was terrified when it saw the fox.

territory   land that belongs to one country or person

terror   great fear

test   **1** questions you have to answer to show how good you are at something
a spelling test
2 to try out
Test the brakes.

tether   to tie an animal up so that it has room to move about, but cannot get away

than   compared with another person or thing
You are smaller than me.

thank   to tell someone you are pleased about something they have given you or done for you

thankful   wanting to thank someone for what they have done

that   the one there
That is mine, this is yours.
Those books are yours.

thatch   straw or reeds used for covering a roof

thaw   **1** to make ice or snow melt
She thawed some snow to get water.
2 the melting of ice or snow
At last the thaw began.

theatre   a place where people go to see plays and shows

theft   stealing
the theft of the diamond

their   belonging to them
their coats

them   see **they**

themselves   **1** they and no one else
2 by themselves   on their own

then   **1** after that
2 at that time
We didn't know about it then.

there   in that place or to that place
Stand there!

therefore   and so

thermometer   an instrument that measures temperature
The thermometer showed how hot it was.

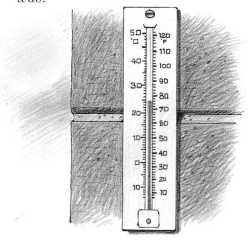

these   see **this**

they   the people or things you are talking about
They all like cake.
I gave each of them a sweet.

thick   measuring a lot from one side to the other
a thick slice of cake

thicken   1 to make thicker
She thickened the gravy with flour.
2 to get thicker
The mixture will thicken when you boil it.

thief   someone who steals things
Ali Baba and the forty thieves

thigh   the top part of the leg down to the knee

thimble   a metal or plastic cover for the end of a finger. You wear it when you sew to protect your finger from the needle.

thin   not fat or thick

thing   anything that can be seen or touched

think   1 to use your mind
2 to have an idea
I thought you were wrong.

third   1 one of the three equal parts something can be divided into. It can also be written as ⅓.
2 coming after the second
third prize

thirst   the feeling that you want to drink

thirsty   wanting a drink
After the race she was thirsty.

this   the one here
This is mine, that is yours.
These books are mine.

thistle   a wild plant with prickly leaves and purple flowers

thorn   a sharp, pointed part on a plant's stem. Roses have thorns.

thorough   1 done properly and carefully
thorough work
2 complete
a thorough mess

those   see **that**

though   and yet, or although
It was very cold though it didn't snow.

thought 1 see **think**
2 something that you think

thoughtful 1 thinking a lot
2 thinking kindly about others
and what they would like

thrash to keep hitting someone with
a stick

thread 1 a long, thin piece of
cotton, nylon, or wool used for
sewing or weaving cloth
2 to put thread through the eye of
a needle or the hole in a bead

threat a promise that you will do
something bad if what you want
does not happen

threaten to make threats

thresh to get the seeds out of corn by
beating it

threw see **throw**

thrifty careful with money

thrill a sudden excited feeling

thrilling very exciting

throat the front of the neck and the
tube inside it that takes foods,
liquid, and air into the body

throb to beat heavily. Your heart
throbs when you have been
running very fast.

throne a special chair for a king or
queen

throttle to kill someone by
squeezing their throat until they
cannot breathe

through from one end or side to the
other
We went through the tunnel.

throughout all through
It was hot throughout the day.

throw to make something move
through the air
*He threw a stone and smashed the
window.*
Jonah was thrown into the sea.

thrush a bird that has a white front
with brown spots on it

thrust to push hard
*He thrust his sword into the
monster and killed it.*

thud to make the low, dull sound
something heavy and large makes
when it hits the ground

thumb the short, thick finger at the
side of each hand

thump to hit hard with the fist

thunder the loud noise that you
hear after a flash of lightning in a
storm

thunderstorm a storm with
thunder and lightning

tick **1** to make the sound some clocks or watches keep making when they are working
2 a small mark like this √

ticket a piece of paper or card that you buy so that you can travel on a bus or train or get into places like cinemas and theatres

tickle to keep touching part of someone's body lightly with your fingers or a feather. Most people laugh when they are tickled.

tide the movement of the sea towards the land and away from the land

tidy neatly arranged with nothing out of place
a tidy room

tie **1** to fasten something with a knot or bow
He's tying it up with ribbon.
2 a long strip of material tied round the collar of a shirt so that the ends hang down the front

tiger a big wild cat found in India and China. It has yellow fur with black stripes.

tight fitting very closely
tight shoes, a tight lid

tighten **1** to make tighter
He tightened the screw with the screwdriver.
2 to get tighter
The rope tightened as the boat moved away.

tights a piece of clothing that fits closely over the feet, legs, and lower part of the body. Women and girls wear tights.
a pair of tights

tile a thin piece of baked clay or something else that is stiff, used in covering a roof, wall, or floor

tiles

till **1** until
She waited till the rain had stopped.
2 a drawer or box for money in a shop
The assistant put the money in the till.

tilt to make something slope
Don't tilt the table.

timber wood that can be used for making things

time **1** seconds, minutes, hours, days, weeks, months, and years
2 a certain moment in the day
What time is it? It's time for tea.
3 the rhythm and speed of a piece of music

timid not brave
The timid mouse hid at the back of the cage.

tingle to sting a little bit
Her ears were tingling with the cold.

tinkle   to make the light, ringing sound a small bell makes

tinsel   thin, shiny, silver ribbon. Tinsel is used for decorating things at Christmas.

tiny   very small

tip   1 the part right at the end of something
2 a small gift of money given to someone for their help
3 a place where rubbish is left
4 to turn something over so that the things inside it fall out

tiptoe   to walk on your toes without making a sound
She tiptoed away.

tired   1 needing to rest or sleep
2 bored with something
I'm tired of work.

tissue   very thin, soft paper

title   1 the name of a book, film, picture, or piece of music
2 a word like Sir, Lady, Dr., Mr., and Mrs. that is put in front of a person's name

titter   to laugh in a silly way

toad   an animal like a big frog. It has rough, dry skin and lives on land.

toadstool   a plant that looks like a mushroom. Most toadstools are poisonous.

toast   bread cooked until it is crisp and brown
beans on toast

tobacco   a plant with leaves that are dried and smoked in pipes or used to make cigars and cigarettes

toboggan   a kind of sledge used for sliding down slopes covered in snow

today   this day

toddler   a young child just beginning to walk

toe   one of the five separate parts at the end of each foot

toffee   butter and sugar cooked together and made into sticky sweets

together   1 with another
joined together
2 at the same time as another
They sang together.

toil   to do hard work

toilet   a lavatory

token   a round piece of plastic or a kind of ticket, used instead of money to pay for something
bus tokens, record tokens

told   see **tell**

tomahawk   an axe once used by American Indians

tomato   a soft, round, red fruit with seeds inside it. Tomatoes can be eaten raw in salads.

tomb   (*rhymes with* room)
a place where a dead person's body is buried. Some tombs are above the ground.

tomorrow   the day after today

ton a large measure for weight

tone 1 a musical sound
2 the kind of sound someone's voice has
a gentle tone

tongs a tool used for getting hold of something and picking it up

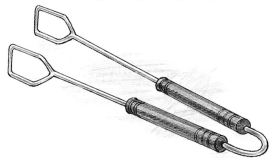

tongue the long, soft, pink part that moves about inside the mouth

tonight this evening or night

tonne a large measure for weight
1 tonne = 1000 Kilograms

tonsils parts of the throat that sometimes cause an illness called **tonsillitis**

too 1 as well
Can I come too?
2 more than is needed
too much

took see **take**

tool something that you use to help you to do a job. Hammers and saws are tools.

tooth one of the hard, white parts in the mouth
Brush your teeth after every meal.

toothache a pain in a tooth

toothbrush a small brush with a long handle, for cleaning teeth

toothpaste a thick paste put on a toothbrush and used for cleaning teeth

topic something interesting that you are writing or talking about

topple to fall over because there is too much on top

topsy-turvy turned upside-down

torch an electric light that you can carry about with you

tore see **tear**²

torment to keep bothering or annoying someone or something for fun, although it is cruel

torn see **tear**²

torpedo a kind of long, round bomb sent under water to destroy ships and submarines
two torpedoes

torrent a very fast stream of water

tortoise a creature with four legs and a shell over its body, that moves slowly

torture 1 great pain that seems as if it will never end
The pain of the toothache was torture.
2 to make someone feel great pain
The bully tortured the little animal by tying up its legs.

toss to throw into the air

total the amount when you have added everything up

totter to walk very shakily as if you are going to fall over. Young children totter when they are learning to walk.

touch 1 to feel something with part of your body
2 to be so close to something else that there is no space in between

tough 1 strong
tough shoes, a tough fighter
2 hard to chew
tough meat

tour 1 a journey you make to visit different places
2 to walk round a place looking at different things

tow to pull along with a rope or chain

toward, towards in the direction of something
He walked towards the school.

towel a piece of cloth for drying things that are wet
a bath towel, a tea towel

tower 1 a tall, narrow building
Blackpool Tower
2 a tall, narrow part of a building
a church tower

town a place with schools, shops, offices, factories, and a lot of houses built near each other

towpath a path beside a canal or river

toy something you play with

trace 1 a mark left by something
2 to copy a picture using thin paper that you can see through. You put the paper over the picture and follow its lines with a pencil.

track 1 a kind of path
2 a railway line
3 to follow the marks left by a person or animal

tractor a machine with wheels and an engine that is used on farms to pull heavy things

trade buying and selling
Our country does a lot of trade with other countries.

traffic cars, buses, bicycles, lorries, and other things travelling on the road

tragedy 1 something very sad that has happened
It was a tragedy that the dog was run over.
2 a play with a very sad ending

trail 1 a rough path
2 smells and marks left behind by an animal. People follow trails when they are hunting.
3 to be dragged along the ground
Your scarf is trailing in the mud.

trailer   something that is pulled along by a car or lorry

train   **1** railway coaches joined together and pulled by an engine
2 to teach a person or animal how to do something
3 to practise for a competition or game

traitor   someone who gives away a secret or gives information about their friends or country to the enemy

tramp   **1** someone without a home or job who walks from place to place
2 to walk heavily

trample   to spoil something by walking heavily on it
The clumsy cattle trampled on the flowers.

trampoline   a large piece of canvas joined to a metal frame with springs for bouncing up and down on

trance   a kind of sleep

transfer   to move someone or something to another place
He was transferred to a different team.

transform   to make a great change in a person or thing
The caterpillar is transformed into a butterfly.

transistor radio   a kind of radio that you can carry about with you easily

transparent   so clear that you can see through it. Glass is transparent.

transport   to take people, animals, or things from one place to another

trap   **1** something made for catching an animal and keeping it prisoner
2 to catch a person or animal by using a trap or a clever trick
They trapped the mouse by using cheese as bait.

trapdoor   a kind of door in the floor or ceiling

trapeze   a bar hanging from ropes, used by acrobats

travel   to go from one place to another

trawler   a fishing boat that pulls a large net along the bottom of the sea

tray   a flat piece of wood or tin used for carrying food, cups, plates, and other light things

treacherous   not to be trusted
The treacherous guard killed the king.

treacle   a thick, sweet, sticky liquid. Treacle is eaten on bread and used in making cakes and puddings.

tread to walk on something
He trod on his glasses and broke them.
They've trodden on the flowers

treason giving away your country's secrets to the enemy

treasure gold, silver, jewels, or other valuable things

treat 1 to behave towards someone or something in a certain way
The horse had been badly treated.
2 to pay for another person's food or drink
My uncle treated us to lunch in a restaurant.
3 something special that pleases you very much
a birthday treat

tree any tall plant with leaves, branches, and a thick stem of wood (See picture on p. 219)

tremble to shake because you are cold or frightened

tremendous very large or great

trench a long, narrow hole dug in the ground

trespass to go on someone else's land, without asking them if you can

trial 1 trying something out to see how well it works
2 the time when a prisoner is in court. The people there decide whether or not he has done something wrong.

triangle a flat shape with three straight edges and three corners (See the list of shapes on p. 223)

tribe a group of families who live together and are ruled by a chief

trick 1 something very clever that a person or animal has learnt to do
2 to make someone believe something that is not true

trickle to move like a very small stream of water

tricycle a machine with three wheels and two pedals that is ridden by young children

tried see **try**

trifle cake and fruit covered in jelly, custard, and cream

trigger the part of a gun that is pulled to fire it

trim 1 to cut away the extra parts of something to make it neat and tidy
2 to decorate a piece of clothing
a coat trimmed with fur

trio a set of three people or things

trip 1 a short journey
a school trip
2 to fall over something
I tripped over and broke my leg.

triumphant very pleased because you have been successful
a triumphant smile

trod, trodden see **tread**

trolley 1 a small, narrow table on wheels
2 a kind of basket on wheels used in supermarkets

troop   an organized group of soldiers or Scouts

tropical   belonging to the very hot countries in Africa, Asia, and South America
tropical plants

trot   one of the ways a horse can move. It is faster than a walk but slower than a canter.

trouble   **1** something that upsets, worries, or bothers you
2 *to take trouble over something* to take great care when you are doing something

trough   (*say* troff)
a long, narrow container that holds food or water for farm animals
a pig trough, a horse trough

trousers   a piece of clothing that covers the body from the waist to the ankles and has separate parts for the legs
a pair of trousers

trout   a fish found in rivers and lakes

trowel   a small spade with a short handle

truant   a pupil who stays away from school without permission

truck   **1** a kind of lorry
2 a cart pulled by a railway engine, for carrying things

trudge   to walk slowly and heavily because you are tired

true   correct or real
a true story, a true friend

truly   in a true or honest way

trumpet   a brass musical instrument that is blown

trunk   **1** a tree's thick stem
2 an elephant's long nose
3 a large box with a lid and handle for carrying things on a journey or storing things

trust   to believe that someone or something will not let you down

truth   something that is true

try   **1** to work at something you want to be able to do
2 to test something
I tried it out before I bought it.

tub   a round container
a tub of ice cream

tube   **1** a long, thin, round container
a tube of toothpaste
2 a long, thin, hollow piece of plastic, rubber, glass, or metal. Tubes are used for taking water and gas from one place to another.

tuck   **1** to tidy away the loose ends of something
She tucked her blouse into her skirt.
2 *tucked up* warm and comfortable in bed

tuft a number of feathers, hairs, or blades of grass growing together

tug **1** to pull hard
He tugged at the rope and broke it.
2 a boat used for pulling ships

tulip a spring flower that grows from a bulb and is shaped like a cup

tumble to fall

tumbler a glass with a flat bottom
a tumbler of water

tune a series of notes that make a piece of music
Listen to the tune and then try to sing it yourself.

tunic **1** a dress worn over a shirt
2 a kind of long jacket worn as part of a uniform
The soldier's tunic had medals pinned on it.

tunnel a long hole that has been made under the ground or through a hill

turban a covering for the head made by wrapping cloth around it in a special way

turbine a kind of engine with a wheel inside it turned by gas, water, or steam

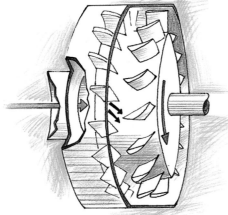

turf short grass and the soil it is growing in

turkey a large bird kept for its meat

turn **1** to move round
2 to change
The prince turned into a frog.
3 to become
She turned pale.
4 a time for you to do something that the others have done or are still waiting to do
It's his turn to set the table.

turnip a round, white vegetable eaten in the winter

turntable the part of a record-player that you put the record on

turpentine a kind of oil that can be used for cleaning paint brushes and mixed with paint to make it thinner

turret a small tower in a castle

turtle a sea creature that looks like a tortoise

tusk one of the two long, pointed teeth an elephant has

tweed warm cloth woven from wool
a tweed coat

tweezers a small tool for getting hold of very thin things such as stamps
a pair of tweezers

twice two times

twig a small, thin branch

twilight the dim light at the end of the day before it gets completely dark

twin one of two children born to the same mother at the same time

twine thin, strong string

twinkle to shine with a lot of tiny flashes of bright light. Stars twinkle.

twirl to turn round and round quickly

twist 1 to turn or bend
a twisted ankle
2 to wrap things round each other

twitch to keep making quick movements with part of the body. Rabbits twitch their noses.

twitter to keep making quick, light sounds like a bird

type 1 one kind or sort
That bird is a type of duck.
2 to write with a typewriter
He typed a letter.

typewriter a machine with keys that you press in order to print letters and numbers

tyre a circle of rubber round the rim of a wheel

U u

ugly not pleasant to look at
the ugly sisters

umbrella a round piece of cloth stretched over a frame that can be opened and shut. You hold an umbrella over your head to keep off the rain.

umpire someone who makes sure that the rules are kept in games such as cricket and tennis

uncle your aunt's husband or the brother of one of your parents

uncomfortable not comfortable
Her tight shoes hurt her feet and were very uncomfortable.

unconscious (*say* un-kon-shuss) in a very deep sleep
After the accident he was unconscious for a week.

under below

underground 1 under the ground
2 a railway that runs through tunnels under the ground
the London Underground

undergrowth bushes and other plants growing under tall trees

underline to draw a straight line underneath a word

underneath in a place under something

understand to know what something means or how it works
He understood what the Frenchman said.

underwear clothes made to be worn under other clothes

undo   to open something that has been fastened with a knot or a button
I undid the knot and opened the parcel.
Your shoe is undone.

undress   to take clothes off

unemployment   when there are not enough jobs for the people who want to work

uneven   not smooth or level

unexpected   not expected
I had an unexpected letter from an old friend.

unfair   not right or just
an unfair game

ungrateful   not grateful
The ungrateful child never thanked them for the present.

unhappy   not happy

unhealthy   not healthy

unicorn   an imaginary animal. It is like a horse, but has a long, straight horn growing out of the front of its head.

uniform   the special clothes that everyone in a group wears so that they look smart together
a school uniform

union   a group of workers who have joined together to make sure that everyone is treated fairly by the people in charge

unique   very unusual because it is the only one of its kind
a unique painting

unit   **1** the number one
hundreds, tens, and units
2 an amount used in measuring or counting. Centimetres are units of length and pence are units of money.

unite   to join together to make one

universal   having to do with everyone and everything

universe   all the worlds that there are and everyone and everything in them

university   a place where some people go to study when they have left school

unkind   not kind

unless   if not

unlike   not like

unload   **1** to take off the things that an animal, boat, car, or lorry is carrying
They unloaded the ship at the dock.
2 to take the bullets out of a gun

unlock   to open a door or box with a key

unlucky   not lucky

unnecessary   not necessary
It is unnecessary to wear your glasses when you're asleep.

unpleasant   not pleasant
The smell of the rubbish was most unpleasant.

unruly   badly behaved and difficult to control

untidy   not tidy

until   up to a certain time
I stayed up until midnight.

unusual   not usual

unwell   ill

unwrap   to take something out of the paper it is wrapped in

upon   on or on top of

upper   higher
the upper lip

upright   **1** standing straight up
an upright post
2 honest
an upright person

uproar   loud noise made by people who are angry or excited about something

upset   **1** to make someone unhappy
2 to knock over
I upset the pot and spilt the paint.

upside-down   turned over so that the bottom is at the top

upstairs   the part of a house that you get to by climbing the stairs

upward, upwards   moving to somewhere higher

urge   **1** to try to make someone hurry to do something
2 a sudden, strong wish to do something
On the mountain he had an urge to fly like a bird.

urgent   so important that it needs to be answered or done at once
an urgent message, urgent work

use   to do a job with something
I used paper and glue to make it.

useful   **1** able to be used a lot
a useful tool
2 helpful
useful information

useless   not useful
A car is useless without petrol.

usual   happening most often
Dinner is at the usual time.

utensil   any tool, pot, or pan used in the kitchen

V v

vacant   with nobody in it
a vacant room

vaccination   (*say* vak-si-nation) an injection that stops you getting an illness

vacuum cleaner   a machine that sucks up dust and dirt from floors and carpets

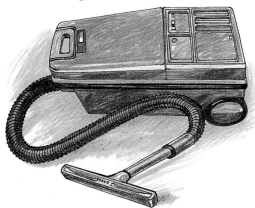

vague   not clear or certain
a vague idea

vain   **1** too proud of yourself and how you look
2 *in vain* without success
They tried in vain to save his life.

valley   low land between hills

valuable   worth a lot of money
valuable jewellery

value   **1** the amount of money something could be sold for
2 how important or useful something is

valve   a part in a machine that makes air, liquid, or electricity go in only one direction

vanilla   the flavour that white ice cream has

vanish   to go away suddenly and not be seen any more

vanity   being too proud of yourself

vapour   steam, mist, or smoke are all vapours. Other vapours are invisible.

variety   **1** a lot of different kinds of things
a variety of flavours
2 a certain sort
That shop sells twenty varieties of ice-cream.

various   different

varnish   a clear liquid painted on to wood or metal to make it shiny

vary   to be different
varied colours

vase   a jar for holding flowers

vast   very large

veal   meat from a calf

vegetable   part of a plant used as food. Vegetables are usually eaten with the main part of a meal. (See picture on p. 217)

vegetarian   (*say* vej-et-air-ee-an) a person who does not eat meat

vehicle   anything that takes people or things from one place to another on land. Cars, vans, buses, bicycles, trains, carts, and lorries are all vehicles.

veil   a piece of thin material used to cover the face or head

vein   one of the narrow tubes inside the body, that carry blood to the heart

velvet   thick material that is smooth and soft on one side
a velvet dress

venom   the poison of snakes

ventilator   a kind of opening in the wall of a room for letting in fresh air

veranda   a long, open place with a roof built on to the side of a house

veranda

verb   any of the words that tell you what someone or something is doing. *Come, go, sit, eat, sleep,* and *think* are all verbs.

verge   grass growing along the edge of a road or path

verse   part of a poem or song

version   a story about something that has happened
His version of the accident is different from mine.

vertical   upright
You can't climb that cliff – it's almost vertical!

very   most
Ice is very cold.

vessel   any container for liquid

vest   a piece of underwear worn on the top half of the body

vet   someone whose job is to help animals that are ill or hurt to get better

viaduct   a long bridge that is a row of arches with a railway or road along the top of it

vicar   someone who serves God by being in charge of a church

vicious   (*say* vish-uss)
bad and cruel
a vicious kick, a vicious temper

victim   someone who has been hurt, robbed, or killed

victory   the winning of a fight or game

video   the recording on special tape of pictures and sound to be played on a television screen

video game   an electronic game which is played on a television screen

videotape recorder   a machine that uses special tape to make copies of television programmes so that they can be watched again later

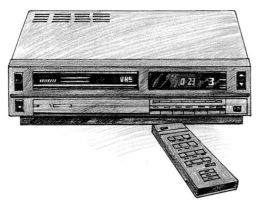

view   1 everything that can be seen from one place
2 what a person thinks about something
My view is that school holidays are too short.

vigour   strength

vile   very nasty
a vile smell

village   a group of houses together with a church and other buildings, in the country

villain   a bad man

vine   a plant that bunches of grapes grow on

vinegar   a sour liquid put on food to make it taste better. People put salt and vinegar on chips.

violent   very strong and rough
a violent storm

violet   1 a tiny purple or white flower that grows in spring
2 purple

violin   a musical instrument made of wood with strings across it that are played with a bow

visibility   how clearly something can be seen. In fog visibility is poor.

visible   able to be seen

vision   1 the ability to see
Glasses will improve your vision.
2 a kind of dream
He saw things in a vision and he thought they were real.

visitor   someone who goes to see a person or place

vivid   **1** bright
vivid colours
2 lively
a vivid imagination
3 so clear it seems real
a vivid dream

vixen   a female fox

vocabulary   a list of the words someone uses

voice   the sound you make with your mouth when you are speaking or singing

volcano   a mountain that contains hot liquid, gases, and ash that sometimes burst out of it
two volcanoes

volume   **1** the amount of space filled by something.
The volume of something is its length × its breadth × its height.
2 one of a set of books
The encyclopedia has ten volumes.
3 how loud a sound is
Turn down the volume on your radio.

volunteer   someone who offers to do something that they do not have to do

vote   to say which person or idea you think should be chosen. Sometimes people vote by putting up their hands and sometimes by making a mark on a piece of paper.

voucher   a printed paper you can use instead of money for buying certain things
a gift voucher

vow   to make a serious promise
The Cub Scouts made a vow to do their best.

vowel   any one of the letters, a, e, i, o, u, and sometimes y

voyage   a long journey by boat

vulture   a large bird that eats dead animals

W w

waddle   to walk like a duck. Ducks take very short steps and move their bodies from side to side.

wade   to walk through water

wafer   a very thin biscuit. Ice cream often has wafers with it.

wag   to move quickly from side to side
The dog wagged its tail.

wage, wages   the money paid to someone for the job they do

wagon   a cart with four wheels that is pulled by horses and used for moving heavy things

wail   to make a long, sad cry

waist   the narrow part in the middle of the body

waistcoat   a short jacket without sleeves or a collar

wait   to stay for something that you are expecting to happen

waiter a man who brings food to people in cafés, hotels, and restaurants

waitress a woman who brings food to people in cafés, hotels, and restaurants

wake to stop sleeping
Wake up!
He woke suddenly and saw the thief.
I was woken by the noise.

walk to move along on foot

walkie-talkie a kind of radio that is carried about and can be used like a telephone

walkie-talkies

wall 1 a barrier made of bricks or stone put round a garden or field
2 one of the sides of a building or room

wallet a small, flat, leather case for money and papers that is carried in the pocket

walnut a kind of nut with a hard shell

waltz a kind of dance done with a partner

wand a thin stick used for casting magic spells. In stories fairies and wizards have wands.

wander to move about without trying to get anywhere
They wandered in the wood picking flowers.

want 1 to feel that you would like to have something
I want a new coat.
2 to need
That car wants washing.

war a fight between countries

ward a bedroom for patients in a hospital

wardrobe a cupboard where clothes are hung

warehouse a large building in which things are stored

warm fairly hot
a warm room

warn to tell someone that they are in danger

warren an area of ground where a lot of rabbits live

warrior someone fighting in a battle

wart a dry, hard spot on the skin

wash to make something clean with water

washing clothes that need washing or are being washed

washing-machine a machine that washes clothes

wasp an insect that flies and can sting

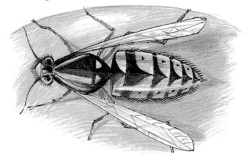

waste   **1** to use more of something than you need to
2 things that you get rid of because you do not need them any more
waste paper

watch   **1** to look at
2 a small clock that is worn or carried

watchman   someone whose job is to guard a building at night

water   the clear liquid in rivers and seas. It falls from the sky as rain.

waterfall   a stream of water falling from a high place to a low place

waterproof   made of material that does not let water through
a waterproof coat

watertight   made so that water cannot get into it
watertight boots

wave   **1** one of the lines of water you can see moving on the surface of the sea
2 to move your hand to say hello or goodbye to someone
Look, she's waving to you.
3 to move up and down or from side to side
The branches waved in the wind.

wavy   with curves in it
wavy hair, a wavy line

wax   something that melts very easily and is used for making candles, crayons, and polish. Some wax is made by bees and some is made from oil.

way   **1** a road or path
This is the way to the beach.
2 how something is done
This is the way to plait hair.

weak   not strong
a weak person, weak tea

weaken   **1** to get weaker
The sick bird weakened each day.
2 to make weaker
Put more water in the squash if you want to weaken it.

wealth   a lot of money or treasure

wealthy   rich

weapon   something used to hurt another person in a fight

wear   **1** to be dressed in something
I wore that dress last time.
2 *to wear out* to become weak and useless because it has been used so much
3 *to wear someone out* to make someone very tired
He was worn out after the match.

weary   very tired

weasel   a small, furry animal with a long body. It kills and eats mice, rats, and rabbits.

weather   rain, snow, ice, fog, wind, and sun

weave   to make material by pushing a thread under and over other threads
She made a loom and wove a scarf on it.
The bag was woven in straw.

web   a thin, sticky net spun by a spider to trap insects

web-foot a foot with its toes joined together by skin. Ducks, otters, and other animals that swim a lot have web-feet.

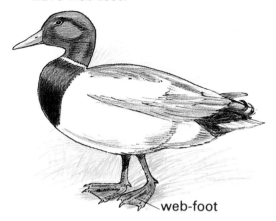

web-foot

wedding the time when a man and woman get married

wedge to keep two things apart by pushing something between them

weed any wild plant that grows where it is not wanted

week the seven days from Sunday to the next Saturday

weekend Saturday and Sunday

weep to let tears fall from the eyes
He wept because he was lost.

weigh 1 to find the weight of something
She weighed the apples on the scales.
2 to have a certain weight
What does that bag of potatoes weigh?

weight 1 how heavy something is
What is your weight?
2 a round piece of metal put on the scales when something is being weighed
Put the 2lb weight on the scales.

weird (*rhymes with* beard)
very strange

welcome to show that you are pleased when someone or something arrives

welfare the health and happiness of people
The doctor was interested in the welfare of his patients.

well 1 healthy
2 in a good way
He swims well.
3 a hole dug to get water or oil out of the ground

wellingtons rubber boots that keep the feet and part of the legs dry
a pair of wellingtons

went see **go**

wept see **weep**

west in the direction of the setting sun

western 1 from the west or in the west
2 a cowboy film

whack to hit hard with a stick

whale the largest sea animal there is

wharf   a place where ships are loaded and unloaded

what   **1** which thing
What is that?
2 that which
Tell me what you think.

whatever   no matter what
Whatever happens, I'll help you.

wheat   a plant grown by farmers. Its seed is used for making flour. (See picture on p. 218)

wheel   **1** a circle of wood or metal fixed in the middle so that it can keep turning round. Cars, bicycles, carts, and some machines have wheels.
2 to push a bicycle, pram, or cart
Do not cycle here, wheel your bike instead.

wheelbarrow   a small cart with one wheel at the front, that is pushed

when   **1** at what time
When are you coming?
2 at the time that
When I moved, it flew away.

whenever   at any time

where   in what place
Where are you?

wherever   no matter where
Wherever you are, I'll find you.

whether   if
She asked whether I could come.

which   what person or thing
Which do you want?

while   in the time that something else is happening
He fell asleep while the television was on.

whimper   the soft sound an animal makes when it is frightened or hurt

whine   the long, sad sound a dog makes when it is unhappy

whip   **1** a long piece of rope or leather joined to a handle and used for hitting things
2 to stir cream hard to make it thick
whipped cream

whirl   to turn round and round very quickly

whisk   **1** to move very quickly
The nurse whisked away the bandage.
2 to stir hard
He whisked the cake mixture.

whisker   a strong hair that grows on the faces of men and animals. A cat has long whiskers growing at each side of its mouth.

whisky   a drink for adults which uses corn or potatoes to make alcohol

whisper   to speak very softly

whistle   **1** to make a shrill sound by blowing through the lips
2 something that makes a shrill sound when it is blown

Whit Sunday   the seventh Sunday after Easter. It is also called **Whitsun**.

who   what person
Who did that?

whoever   no matter what person
Whoever did it will be in trouble.

whole **1** not broken
Swallow it whole.
2 all of something
the whole world

whooping-cough (*say* hooping cough)
an illness that makes you keep coughing and breathing in heavily

whose belonging to what person
Whose is this?

why because of what
Why did you do that?

wick the string that goes through the middle of a candle, which you light

wicked very bad
a wicked witch

wicket the set of three stumps with two bails on top of them in cricket

bails

wicket

stumps

wide **1** measuring a lot from one side to the other
2 completely
wide awake, wide open

widow a woman whose husband has died

widower a man whose wife has died

width how wide something is

wife a woman married to someone
Henry VIII had six wives.

wig a covering of false hair worn on the head

wigwam the kind of tent American Indians used to live in

wild **1** not looked after by people
a wild flower
2 not controlled
a wild horse, a wild temper

wilderness wild land where no one lives

wilful wanting to do something, even though other people say it is wrong
a wilful child

will **1** instructions left by a person who has died telling people what they want to be done with their money and things
2 the power to choose what you want to do
3 is going to
He will be nine tomorrow.
We'll soon be there.
I said I would be late.
I'd like another cake.

willing ready and happy to do what is wanted

willow a kind of tree that grows near water and has thin branches that bend easily. Its wood is used for making cricket bats.
(See picture on p. 219)

wily crafty

win **1** to get a prize
2 to beat someone else in a game or fight
We've won four matches and lost two.

wince   to move slightly because you are upset or in pain

wind[1]   (*rhymes with* grinned) air moving along quickly

wind[2]   (*rhymes with* blind)
1 to turn a key to make a machine work
The clock started when she wound it up.
2 to wrap cloth, thread, tape, or string tightly round something

windmill   a mill that uses wind to make its machinery work.

window   an opening in the wall of a building. It is filled with glass and lets in light.

wine   a strong drink make from grapes

wing   one of the parts of a bird or insect used for flying
a pair of wings

wink   to close and open one eye quickly

winter   the coldest part of the year

wipe   to rub something with a cloth to dry it or clean it

wire   a long, thin strip of metal that can be bent into different shapes

wireless   a radio

wisdom   the ability to understand many things
They say you gain wisdom as you get older.

wise   able to understand many things

wish   to say or think what you would like to happen

wisp   a little bit of straw, hair, or smoke

witch   a woman who uses magic. Witches in fairy stories have tall, black, pointed hats and ride in the air on brooms.

with   **1** having
a man with a wooden leg
2 in the company of
I came with a friend.
3 using
It was written with a pen.
4 against
fighting with the enemy

wither   to dry up and get paler and smaller
withered flowers

without   not having
without any money

witness   someone who sees something important happen
She was a witness to the accident.

witty   clever and funny

wives   more than one wife

wizard   a man in fairy stories, who can do magic things

wobble   to shake or rock. Jelly wobbles.

woke, woken   see **wake**

wolf   a wild animal like a big, fierce dog
a pack of wolves

wolves

woman   a fully grown female
The three women were sisters.

won   see **win**

wonder   **1** a feeling of surprise because of something strange or marvellous
2 to ask yourself about something
I wonder who did it.

wonderful   so good that it surprises you
a wonderful holiday

wood   **1** the branches and trunks of trees cut up so that they can be used for making things or burnt on fires
2 a lot of trees growing together

wooden   made of wood

woodpecker   a bird that eats insects living in tree trunks. It has a strong beak for making holes in wood and a long, sticky tongue for catching insects.

woodwork   making things out of wood
a woodwork lesson

wool   the thick, soft hair that covers sheep. It is spun into thread and used for making cloth and for knitting.

woollen   made of wool

word   a sound or group of sounds that means something when you say it, write it, or read it

word-processor   a computer with a keyboard and a display screen. It will store and display the words that are typed into it from the keyboard.

wore   see **wear**

work   a job or something else that you have to do

workman   a man paid to work with his hands, a tool, or a machine

workshop   a place where things are made or mended

world   the earth or anything else in space that is like it

worm   a long, thin creature that wriggles about in the soil

worn   see **wear**

worry   **1** to be upset because you are thinking about something bad that might happen
2 to get hold of something with the teeth and shake it, as dogs do with slippers

worse   less good
He's a worse swimmer than I am.

worship to love and praise someone
Christians worship God.

worst least good
He's the worst in the class at swimming.

worth with a certain value
This old stamp is worth £100.

worthless not worth anything

would see **will**

wound[1] (*say* woond)
an injury from something like a knife or a bullet

wound[2] (*rhymes with* sound)
see **wind**[2]

wove, woven see **weave**

wrap to put cloth or paper round something

wreath flowers or leaves twisted together into a ring
a holly wreath

wreck 1 to damage a ship, building, or car so badly that it cannot be used again
The earthquake wrecked the building.
2 a ship, building, or car so badly damaged that it cannot be used again
The car was a wreck after the accident.

wren a very small, brown bird

wrestle to struggle with someone

wretched (*say* retch-id)
1 unhappy or ill
2 poor
wretched health

wriggle to twist and turn the body about like a worm

wring to squeeze and twist something wet to get the water out of it

wrinkle a small crease in the skin. Old people usually have a lot of wrinkles.

wrist the thin part of the arm where it is joined to the hand

write to put words or signs on paper so that people can read them
I wrote to her last week.
You have written this very neatly.

writhe to twist or roll about because you are in great pain
The injured dog was writhing in pain and distress.

writing something that has been written
untidy writing
a piece of writing

written see **write**

wrong not right
the wrong answer

wrote see **write**

wrung see **wring**

X x

X-ray a special photograph that shows the inside of a body so that doctors can see if there is anything wrong

xylophone a row of wooden or metal bars that you hit with small hammers to make musical sounds

Y y

yacht (*say* yot)
a light boat with sails, used for racing (See picture on p. 215)

yard 1 a measure for length
2 ground that is next to a building and has a wall round it

yawn to open your mouth wide because you are tired

year a measure for time. A year is twelve months, or three hundred and sixty-five days.

yell to shout

yelp to give a quick, shrill cry like a dog in pain

yesterday the day before today

yew a kind of tree that has dark green leaves it keeps all through the year (See picture on p. 219)

yield 1 to give in
2 the amount of fruit or grain on a plant
a good yield of apples

yodel to shout with a musical sound, changing from a low note to a high note and back again

yoghurt a thick liquid made from sour milk. It usually has fruit in it and you eat it with a spoon.

yolk (*rhymes with* joke)
the round, yellow part of an egg

you the person or people you are speaking to

young born not long ago. A kitten is a young cat.

youngster someone who is young

your belonging to you
your book

yourself, yourselves 1 you and no one else
2 *by yourself, by yourselves* on your own

youth 1 a boy or young man
2 the time in your life when you are young

Z z

zebra an animal like a horse with black and white stripes. Zebras are found in Africa.

zero the number nothing, also written 0

zigzag a line with sudden turns in it like this ∿∿∿

zip, zipper a special fastener for joining two edges of material together. Some dresses, trousers, and bags have zips.

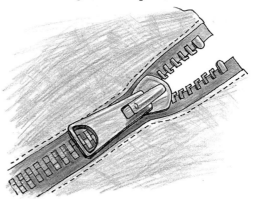

zone a part of a town, country, or the world that is special in some way
a parking zone

zoo a place where different kinds of wild animals are kept so that people can go and see them

zoom to move very quickly

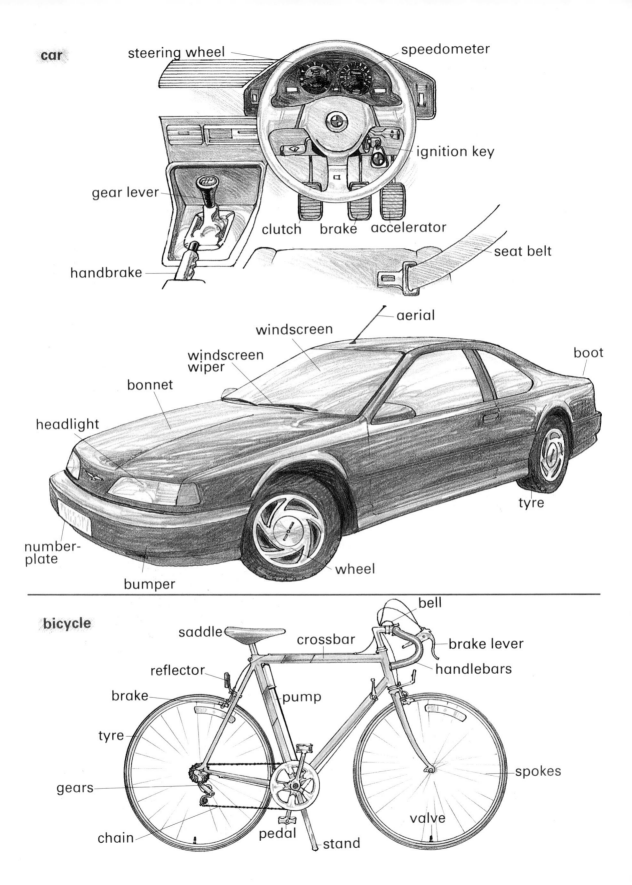

car

steering wheel

speedometer

ignition key

gear lever

clutch brake accelerator

seat belt

handbrake

aerial

windscreen

boot

windscreen wiper

bonnet

headlight

tyre

number-plate

wheel

bumper

bicycle

saddle

bell

crossbar

brake lever

reflector

handlebars

brake

pump

tyre

spokes

gears

valve

chain

pedal stand

ships and boats

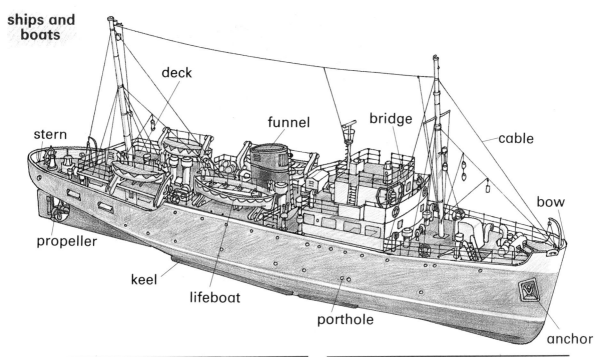

stern

deck

funnel

bridge

cable

propeller

keel

lifeboat

porthole

bow

anchor

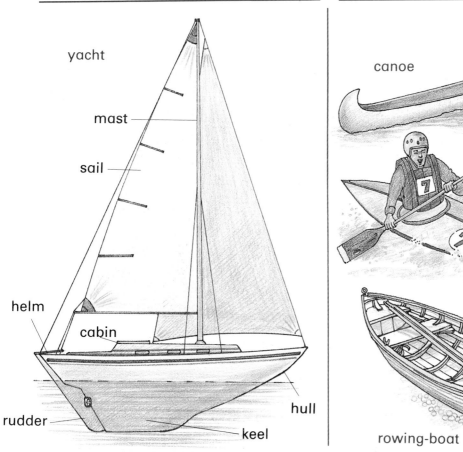

yacht

mast

sail

helm

cabin

rudder

keel

hull

canoe

kayak

rowing-boat

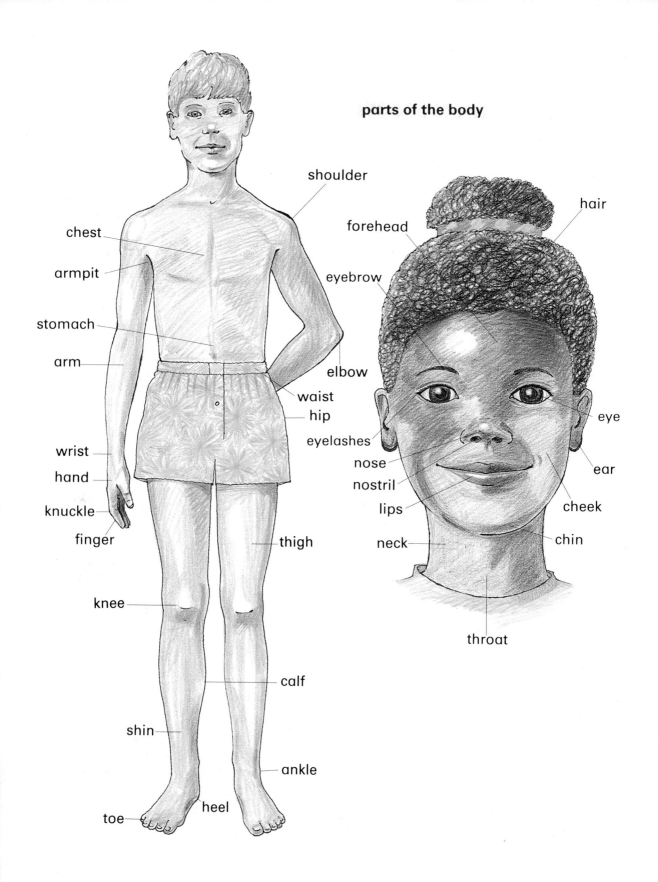

parts of the body

shoulder

chest

armpit

stomach

arm

wrist

hand

knuckle

finger

knee

shin

ankle

toe

heel

thigh

calf

forehead

hair

eyebrow

elbow

waist

hip

eyelashes

nose

nostril

lips

neck

eye

ear

cheek

chin

throat

216

fruits

vegetables

apple

apricot

orange

banana

blackberries

raspberries

gooseberries

plum

cherries

blackcurrants

peach

grapes

lemon

grapefruit

pear

mango

melon

lychees

turnip

radishes

parsnip

potato

carrots

onion

beetroot

peas

cauliflower

cabbage

lettuce

spinach

leek

sweetcorn

celery

Brussels sprouts

broccoli

asparagus

flowers and plants

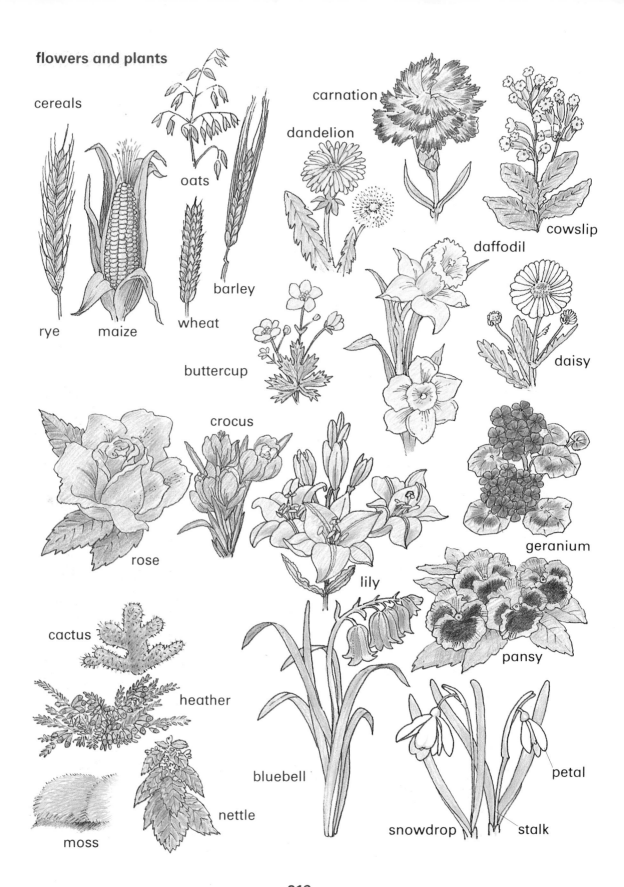

cereals

oats

carnation

dandelion

cowslip

barley

daffodil

wheat

buttercup

daisy

rye   maize

crocus

rose

lily

geranium

pansy

cactus

heather

bluebell

snowdrop

petal

nettle

stalk

moss

trees

leaf

acorn

conker

oak

horse-chestnut

trunk

catkin

willow

beech

poplar

ash

sycamore

cypress

maple

yew

eucalyptus

birch

elm

dogs

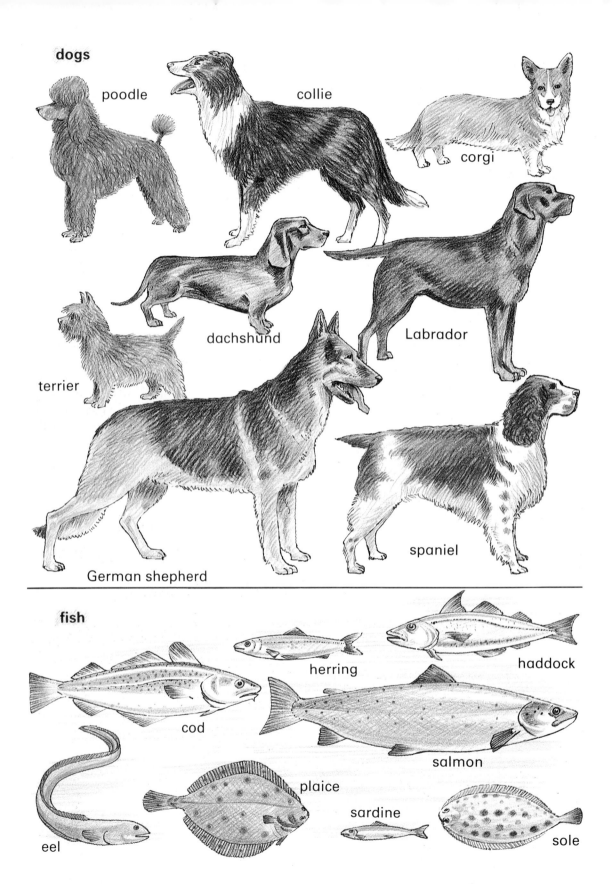

poodle

collie

corgi

dachshund

Labrador

terrier

German shepherd

spaniel

fish

herring

haddock

cod

salmon

plaice

eel

sardine

sole

musical instruments

violin

cello

double-bass

French horn

trumpet

trombone

tuba

piccolo

oboe

flute

clarinet

piano

bassoon

tambourine

triangle and beater

cymbals

scientific equipment

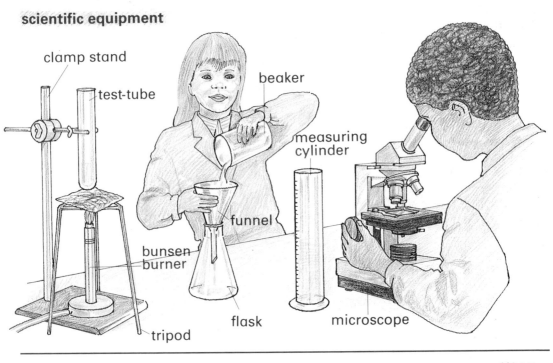

clamp stand

test-tube

beaker

measuring cylinder

funnel

bunsen burner

flask

tripod

microscope

camera

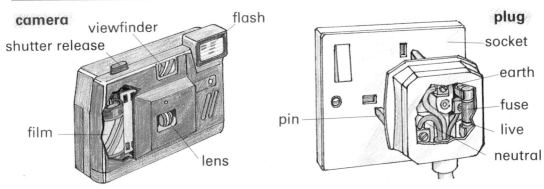

viewfinder

flash

shutter release

film

lens

plug

socket

earth

fuse

live

neutral

pin

playing cards

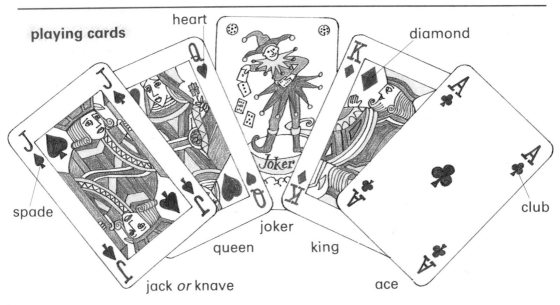

heart

diamond

spade

club

joker

queen

king

jack *or* knave

ace

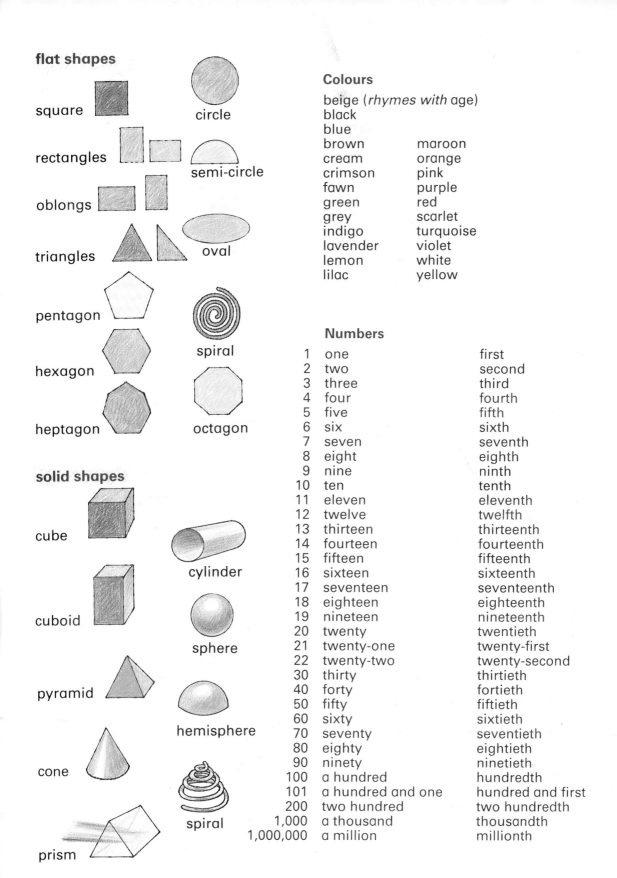

flat shapes

square

circle

rectangles

semi-circle

oblongs

triangles

oval

pentagon

spiral

hexagon

heptagon

octagon

solid shapes

cube

cylinder

cuboid

sphere

pyramid

hemisphere

cone

spiral

prism

Colours

beige (*rhymes with* age)
black
blue

brown	maroon
cream	orange
crimson	pink
fawn	purple
green	red
grey	scarlet
indigo	turquoise
lavender	violet
lemon	white
lilac	yellow

Numbers

1	one	first
2	two	second
3	three	third
4	four	fourth
5	five	fifth
6	six	sixth
7	seven	seventh
8	eight	eighth
9	nine	ninth
10	ten	tenth
11	eleven	eleventh
12	twelve	twelfth
13	thirteen	thirteenth
14	fourteen	fourteenth
15	fifteen	fifteenth
16	sixteen	sixteenth
17	seventeen	seventeenth
18	eighteen	eighteenth
19	nineteen	nineteenth
20	twenty	twentieth
21	twenty-one	twenty-first
22	twenty-two	twenty-second
30	thirty	thirtieth
40	forty	fortieth
50	fifty	fiftieth
60	sixty	sixtieth
70	seventy	seventieth
80	eighty	eightieth
90	ninety	ninetieth
100	a hundred	hundredth
101	a hundred and one	hundred and first
200	two hundred	two hundredth
1,000	a thousand	thousandth
1,000,000	a million	millionth

Continents

Africa
Antarctica
Asia
Australia
Europe
North America
South America

Days

Sunday
Monday
Tuesday
Wednesday
Thursday
Friday
Saturday

Planets

Mercury
Venus
Earth
Mars
Jupiter
Saturn
Uranus
Neptune
Pluto

Months

January
February
March
April
May
June
July
August
September
October
November
December

Places Peoples

Afghanistan Afghans
Africa Africans
Algeria Algerians
America Americans
Argentina Argentinians
Asia Asians
Australia Australians
Austria Austrians
Bangladesh Bangladeshis
Belgium Belgians
Brazil Brazilians
Britain the British
Canada Canadians
Chile Chileans
China the Chinese
Cuba Cubans
Cyprus Cypriots
Czech Republic Czechs
Denmark Danes
Egypt Egyptians
England the English
Ethiopia Ethiopians
Europe Europeans
Finland Finns

France the French
Germany Germans
Ghana Ghanaians
Great Britain *see* **Britain**
Greece Greeks
Holland the Dutch
Hungary Hungarians
Iceland Icelanders
India Indians
Indonesia Indonesians
Ireland the Irish
Israel Israelis
Italy Italians
Jamaica Jamaicans
Japan the Japanese
Jordan Jordanians
Kenya Kenyans
Lapland Lapps
Lebanon the Lebanese
Libya Libyans
Malaysia Malaysians
Malta the Maltese
Mexico Mexicans
Morocco Moroccans
New Zealand New Zealanders
Nigeria Nigerians
Norway Norwegians
Pakistan Pakistanis
Poland Poles
Portugal the Portuguese
Russia Russians
Saudi Arabia Saudi Arabians
Scotland Scots
Slovakia Slovaks
Spain Spaniards
Sri Lanka Sri Lankans
Sweden Swedes
Switzerland the Swiss
Syria Syrians
Tanzania Tanzanians
Thailand Thais
Trinidad Trinidadians
Turkey Turks
Uganda Ugandans
United Kingdom *see* **Britain**
United States of America (USA) Americans
Venezuela Venezuelans
Vietnam the Vietnamese
Wales the Welsh
West Indies West Indians
Zambia Zambians
Zimbabwe Zimbabweans